Root Cellaring
The Ultimate Guide to Building a Root Cellar and Keeping Food in Cold Storage

Table of Contents

Introduction
Chapter 1: An Introduction to Root Cellars
Chapter 2: How Does a Root Cellar Thrive?
Chapter 3: What to Store in a Root Cellar
Chapter 4: Easy DIY Root Cellar Alternatives
Chapter 5: Planning Essentials
Chapter 6: How to Build a Simple Root Cellar
Chapter 7: DIY Shelving Systems for Produce
Chapter 8: 8 Best Methods to Organizing a Root Cellar
Chapter 9: Troubleshooting Common Problems
Chapter 10: Cleaning and Sanitizing a Root Cellar
Conclusion

Introduction

Welcome to the world of root cellaring. Some of you will be lost in nostalgia, remembering your grandparents' and parents' root cellars, while others will be wondering what they even are. The fact that you are reading this book shows that you want to know and are interested in root cellars.

This book will guide you through everything you need to know about the humble root cellar, from its origins right up to modern-day use. By the time you get to the end, you will have a solid plan in mind of what you want to do, how you will achieve it, and when.

This is where the excitement builds. All that fantastic, organic, healthy food you can grow in your garden—you can now store it and live off it all year! Forget buying vegetables wrapped in harmful plastic from the grocery store and food that you know has been sprayed in chemicals or imported from a foreign country at great expense. Instead, think of the rows of carrots and potatoes, the corn, onions, beets, and the dozens of other things you can grow in your garden and put away to live on over the winter.

Run an Internet search for books on root cellars, and you will find quite a few. However, this one is different. This one will teach you how to build a root cellar, not just one you dig into the ground, but how to make one from something else. After all, not everyone has a vast garden and space to start digging down to build a cellar. You might be surprised at what you can use to store your vegetables, and this book lists some exciting ideas for you to try out.

Now, time to dig in. Turn the pages and work your way through this incredibly easy-to-read guide on root cellars and follow the steps outline—you will soon be well on your way to becoming a master at it!

Chapter 1: An Introduction to Root Cellars

Can you imagine what your life would be like without a refrigerator in the kitchen? Since the 1800s, technology has come a long way, and now virtually every household has at least one refrigerator working to keep their food cool and fresh. Imagine not having one. Picture going back to a time way before these cold units were even thought of.
Before the rise of modern, convenient home appliances, most people had a root cellar. Those who did not have one were looked down upon—considered too poor to even have a hole in the ground where they could store food. While root cellars lost ground many years ago, replaced by modern-day luxuries, they were essential in older times. Even as late as World War II people were still using them to keep precious food supplies fresh. Today, root cellars are making a huge comeback. Keep reading to find out what they are and why they are, once again, so popular.

What is a Root Cellar?

Technically, root cellars are rooms below the ground that use the earth's natural humidifying, cooling, and insulating properties. They are an old-fashioned way of storing and preserving food to get people through the winter months. While they were once rooms beneath the house, cellars nowadays are any type of storage that keeps food fresh for longer by controlling light, temperature, and humidity. Your refrigerator is the modern root cellar, but learning how to make a root cellar successfully is essential if you do not want to rely on electricity.
Every root cellar, regardless of design, functions in the same basic way. If properly constructed, it can keep your food up to 40 degrees Fahrenheit cooler than ambient summertime temperatures. During the winter, low temperature also has significant benefits, as storing food at temperatures just above freezing point can slow down rot and deterioration. Even in a basement, the temperatures are slightly warmer inside your homes, meaning stored foods will spoil much quicker. If the temperature rises above 45 degrees Fahrenheit, most vegetables will turn tough, start sprouting, and quickly spoil. That said, root cellar temperatures are never the same in every corner. Near the top, the temperature is around 10 degrees warmer than the lower part of the cellar, so it is important to organize the root cellar efficiently. Place vegetables that tolerate warmer temperatures at the top.
Now, what if your garden is too small or you have no interest in growing your own vegetables? Not a problem—root cellars are designed to store produce that you don't have to grow yourself. If you can pick up great bargains from your local farm or farmer's market, you can just as easily store those in your cellar.

Root cellars were originally designed for root vegetables, which is where their name comes from — vegetables such as potatoes, carrots, parsnips, beets, and turnips are ideal for this type of storage. However, these days, people store much more, including apples, flower bulbs, canned goods, pears, pickled vegetables, etc. Think of a root cellar as a huge extension to your pantry.

A Brief History of the Root Cellar

The root cellar has a long and interesting history, dating back at least 40,000 years. The first to start using the earth's natural insulation and cooling properties to store food were Indigenous Australians. Records show that over 40,000 years ago, they were growing vast amounts of yams and came up with a way of storing it long term, namely burying it in the ground. While developing their technique, they also discovered another process, fermentation, and that is why alcoholic beverages are commonly stored in cellars.
Iron Age storage rooms have also been discovered beneath the ground, which Etruscans still use to store immature wine. Although the first alleged use of a walk-in root cellar occurred in seventeenth century England, the most notable uses came from English colonists who settled in North America.

During ancient times, China and Egypt had already mastered preserving food using methods such as salting, pickling, using spices, and drying. However, cold winters and widespread famines are what drove the British to invent the walk-in root cellar. Across the eastern parts of Canada and America, the land is scattered with old root cellars; thousands of them. Elliston, a small town in Newfoundland, has even claimed the title of "Root Cellar Capital of the World," with over 135 root cellars, some of them around 200 years old.

Pros and Cons of Root Cellaring

Understandably, more and more people are now turning to their gardens to feed themselves, and the humble root cellar is an integral part of this. While you may choose to grow only a small amount and buy the rest from markets, proper storage remains essential. And there are a few reasons why they are suddenly becoming so popular again:

- They cost little to nothing to run. You don't need electricity unless you want a lightbulb in your root cellar.
- You can store your own home-grown produce or stock up on seasonal goods purchased from farmer's markets.
- Your food is guaranteed to be organic and free from the chemicals that most shop-bought vegetables are conventionally sprayed with.
- Recent and ongoing events worldwide have led people to become more self-sufficient. Building simple root cellars helps them get their bounty throughout the year.
- There may come a time when you cannot get to a grocery store to get your food—with a root cellar, you don't have to worry.
- The recent pandemic has shown how quickly people will empty grocery stores without a second thought—if you don't get there in time, there is nothing left. When you have your own produce stored in a root cellar, you can feed yourself and your family with reassurance and comfort.

The Advantages
- You can have food stored seven days a week, 365 days a year
- No electricity is required
- It is a proven food storage method—even our ancestors knew it worked
- They are incredibly versatile—you can have one in any size or shape, and your budget can be as big or as small as you decide

Disadvantages

- You need space—if you have none, this perhaps is not for you
- There are many different types, and each has its pros and cons

What You Need to Know About Root Cellars

What to Store?
As established, root cellars can be used to store just about anything these days. Traditionally, they were used to store root vegetables, mostly potatoes, turnips, and carrots. Today, people store other root vegetables, apples, pears, hard fruits, etc. In addition, you can store canned foods, medicines, salted meat and fish, and so much more. If you build one big enough, you can even use it as an emergency shelter!

How They Function
Root cellars use the earth to maintain good humidity, light, and temperature levels. The optimum temperature is 32 to 40 degrees Fahrenheit, and the optimum humidity is 85 to 95 percent. For a successful root cellar, you need three essential things: humidity, darkness, and good ventilation.

Temperature is incredibly important. If properly controlled, the temperature helps the vegetables and fruits slowly release ethylene gas, allowing microorganisms to grow and stopping the decomposition process in its tracks. In parallel, high humidity prevents moisture from evaporating.

Different Types of Root Cellars
In the olden days, a root cellar was a room built beneath a house or in the ground to store vegetables. Nowadays, just about anything can be used:
- Basements or space under the porch
- Holes dug in the ground
- Old refrigerators or freezers
- Garbage cans
- And much more— all that is required is your imagination!

Common Mistakes When Building Root Cellars

Many people dive straight into building their root cellars without stopping to think about what needs to be done and how to do it. While they are a fantastic idea, they are hard work— even the simplest in design—and there are several things you should consider before you start.
- **Lack of Ventilation**

The most common mistake is not installing ventilation. If your room is airtight, humidity levels can build up very quickly, leading to excess moisture in the room. Ideally, you should have two vents as an absolute minimum, each a few inches in diameter. They should have a mesh screen over them to keep out mice and other unwanted pests, and one should be at the top of the room, helping to vent our ethylene gas and stale air as well. There should be one near the bottom of the room to allow fresh air in. How many you install will depend on how large your root cellar is.

- **Not Enough Light**

When you create a root cellar, you must consider exposure to the light. This must be controlled because light exposure is one of the biggest problems in food storage. There are several reasons for this, including bleaching food, which wipes out its nutritional content and value.

Some vegetables, especially potatoes, will turn green and begin sprouting if they are exposed to light. Therefore, if you opt to have lighting in the cellar, it must be the minimum amount possible, and it should never be left on. You could also cover your vegetables with cardboard or burlap to protect them from light and maintain optimum temperature.

- **Tossing Fruits and Vegetables in Together**

Vegetables and fruits should be kept separate in a root cellar. While they may need pretty much the same conditions for storage, some fruits produce more ethylene gas. In excessive amounts, it can compromise vegetable health and lifespan. Some of these fruits include blueberries, apples, avocados, apricots, bananas, cranberries, citrus fruit, and cantaloupe melons.

Takeaway

If you want a natural method of storing your fruits and vegetables, consider building a root cellar. They may be hard work but are well worth the investment, and the benefits are amazing.

That was a very brief introduction to root cellars. So far, this book has not gone into detail because much of what you have read here will be covered in greater depth later. Thus, without further ado, it is time to get into how root cellars work.

Chapter 2: How Does a Root Cellar Thrive?

Before you can even think about building a root cellar, there are many things to consider. Perhaps the most important thing is working out the conditions needed to store your fruits and vegetables, which all come into your design.

Basically, every root cellar, no matter what design you choose, works on the same principles—staying dark and cool all year and not freezing. Simple enough, right? You can use just about any cool space you have available, such as a space in your garage or basement. Or you can get right down to it and build one in your garden. However, there are two things to consider here. In regions where winters are mild, you may need to provide artificial cooling as the earth may not do the job sufficiently for you. In contrast, if you live where the weather is hot, such as the tundra, you might need additional insulation.

A quick Internet search will provide you with tons of plans in terms of building a root cellar. Do not just pick the first one—all root cellars are different, so it is important to choose the one that works best for you. The key things to consider are size and shape, which will determine how your root cellar thrives. How so? Because the size and shape determine how you deal with humidity and temperature.

The Basics of Root Cellaring

As established, root cellars need to provide three conditions: humidity, ventilation, and temperature. The closer you can get to the ideal conditions, the more success yours will have.

Humidity

Root cellars require high levels of humidity, around 85 to 95 percent. This stops your stored produce from drying out and shriveling up. There are three ways to achieve the right levels of humidity in your root cellar:

- *A dirt floor* — Dirt floors retain moisture much easier than their concrete or stone counterparts. Suppose you built your root cellar into the ground. In that case, you already have an advantage because the soil will provide some humidity. The earth should be packed in solid, and then a layer of gravel placed over the top. This does two things: it keeps your feet dry when things get damp and helps retain moisture. If your cellar does get dry, you can spray a little water (carefully) over the gravel. The water will evaporate quickly, causing more moisture and humidity in the air.

- *Adding water* — If you do not want to add gravel or if your floors are made of concrete, there are other solutions. You can add water by spraying the floor lightly, spreading damp burlap bags over the vegetables (making sure they are not soaking wet), or placing a few pans of water on the floor. Measures like these are usually required in the fall season when you first put your produce into storage. Dug-in root cellars are less likely to require help with humidity, whereas basement root cellars will do. In areas where the air is very moist, you can keep root vegetables in bins, uncovered, so they are kept firm and smooth.
- *Sawdust, moss, or sand* — Now, if your humidity falls below optimum levels, there is a third option. You can use damp sawdust, moss, or sand to pack your fruits and vegetables in. This works especially well for parsnips, beets, and carrots, helping cut down on surface evaporation.

One of the most important things to factor in is that warm air absorbs more moisture than cool air. If your root cellar is damp and cold, the environment will be somewhat unstable. For example, if your air temperature is 34 degrees Fahrenheit, it has room to absorb a bit more moisture. However, if the temperature drops a couple of degrees, the air will become saturated. This is known as the "dew point," where the air can no longer hold excess water. That water will start condensing on your ceiling, walls, and your fruit and vegetables. The safest way to ensure your humidity levels are correct is to invest in a hygrometer — you can get one from any hardware store or garden center.

Ventilation

Equally important to humidity is proper ventilation. Air must be allowed into the cellar and able to circulate through it, keeping the temperature low. Adjusting the air intake is critical to help reduce extra humidity and preventing condensation from destroying all your hard work. When air moves efficiently, it eliminates the ethylene gas some fruits give off and other vegetable odors that could alter flavors in other vegetables and fruit. Understanding how the air circulates through your root cellar requires you to remember basic science — hot air rises (lighter) while cold air falls (heavier). If you have a large or enclosed cellar, you need to have two things: an air intake system and an air outlet. The intake should be situated quite low in the room, bringing in the cool air from outside. The outlet should be higher up, allowing warmer air to escape. It is best to have the outlet and inlet on opposite sides of the room to allow the air to circulate efficiently.

Where your storage area is smaller, or where there are plenty of cracks to allow the air in — think old stone foundations — you may find it is enough to have one outlet situated high up to remove the warm air. When you store your produce, make sure it is elevated off the ground a couple of inches — this allows the air to circulate beneath them.

Temperature

Temperature is, above all else, the vital variable to consider in a root cellar. Good root cellars do two things: they borrow cold, and they stay cold. How do you borrow cold? It is simple — dig into the ground. Below the frost level, the earth will stay at a steady temperature of around 52 degrees. This is because the deeper earth temperature takes much longer to be affected by the freezing temperatures above, offering your vegetables more protection. If you choose not to dig your root cellar into the ground, there are two other ways you can borrow the cold; with a window or an exhaust pipe that you can close off. These options will allow the cold night air into the cellar but should be shut off during the day when the temperatures rise.

Successfully maintain a temperature of 32 to 40 degrees, and you have the perfect place for food storage. If your temperatures are between 40 and 50 degrees, you can still use the root cellar as a short-term storage area for apples and root vegetables. Peppers, eggplant, and tomatoes can be kept for about a month.

Because there is a difference in temperature between the floor and the ceiling, you can take advantage of it by placing your fruits and vegetables per their storage requirements — more on that later.

Invariably, you need to invest in a good thermometer to monitor your root cellar temperatures.

Tips on Keeping Your Root Cellar Cool

Creating the optimum atmosphere can be done by following these simple tips:
- Your root cellar should be dug in about ten feet (or three meters), as this is where temperature stability is reached.
- Do not site a dug-in root cellar near large trees. Not only will you find it difficult to dig through the roots, but eventually, they will grow through your cellar walls.
- Use wooden platforms, bins, and shelves to store your produce on and in. Wood does not conduct the cold or heat as quickly as metal does, and plastic may turn brittle.
- Ensure your shelves are between 1 and 3 inches away from the walls—this ensures good air circulation, minimizing the chances of airborne mold.
- If your root cellar is outdoors, the best flooring is packed earth, whereas, in a basement cellar, concrete is more practical and works better.
- Make sure you have a hygrometer and a thermometer handy and check them every day.
- Use inlets and outlets to regulate heat and cold into and out of the root cellar.

More Tips on Storage and Root Cellar Conditions

- If you need to preserve moisture in your cellar and create a humid micro-climate, place the vegetables that need that climate in individual bags with holes in them. Alternatively, you can use perforated, sealed plastic containers. Avoid regular plastic containers—although they do work for some things.
- Conversely, you can create dry micro-climates using sealed containers with materials that absorb moisture in them. For example, a cup of rice in a paper bag absorbs air moisture while the bag keeps the rice away from your vegetables.
- Start planning your root cellar storage at the start of the planting season. Choose varieties designed for long storage periods.
- When you harvest your vegetables, do not wash them before storing them. The cellar will have disease-fighting properties, and washing it off may be detrimental.
- Conduct enough research—some vegetables need to be cured before storing them, while others store better if exposed to frost. Proper research ensures you get the best lifespan for your produce.
- Do not store anything that is diseased or damaged. If you bruise or cut any vegetable or fruit during the harvest, put it to one side—this should be eaten first.
- Make sure you check your storage every couple of weeks to ensure nothing is going bad. If anything is, remove it immediately before it affects the rest of your harvest.

What a Root Cellar Can Do for You

Having a root cellar ensures that you enjoy vegetables and fruits out of season or produce you cannot get at the grocery store unless sprayed and imported. To achieve this, you do not have to bottle, can, boil, or freeze anything.

What is more, no longer will you be confined to storing only certain vegetables—carrots, potatoes, and turnips. Provided you plan your root cellar program well, you can store all kinds—nuts, fresh tomatoes, cantaloupes, sweet potatoes, and much more.

Don't worry if you find that you can't always fill your root cellar with what you grow. Visit the farmer's markets and purchase in-season vegetables or storage vegetables in the fall.

Here are some of the foods you can store along with useful indications:

Food	Temperature	Humidity	Shelf-Life
Apples	32 degrees F	90 to 95%	Two to seven months, depending on the variety
Dried Beans	50 to 60 degrees F	60 to 70%	One year

Beets	32 degrees	90 to 95%	Three to five months
Broccoli	32 degrees F	90 to 95%	One to two weeks
Brussels Sprouts	32 degrees F	90 to 95%	Three to five weeks
Cabbage	32 degrees F	90 to 95%	Three to four months
Carrots	32 degrees F	90 to 95%	Four to six months
Garlic	50 to 60 degrees F	60 to 70%	Five to eight months
Jerusalem Artichokes	32 degrees F	90 to 95%	One to two months
Leeks	32 degrees F	90 to 95%	Three to four months
Onions	50 to 60 degrees F	60 to 70%	Five to eight months
Parsnips	32 degrees	90 to 95%	One to two months
Pears	30 degrees	90 to 95%	Two to three months
Potatoes	40 to 45 degrees F	90 to 95%	Four to six months
Pumpkins	50 to 60 degrees F	60 to 70%	Five to six months
Rutabagas	32 degrees F	90 to 95%	Two to four months
Squash	50 to 60 degrees F	60 to 70%	Four to six months
Sweet Potatoes	55 to 60 degrees F	60 to 70%	Four to six months
Tomatillos	50 to 60 degrees F	60 to 70%	One to two months
Tomatoes	50 to 60 degrees F	60 to 70%	One to two months—green tomatoes Four to six months for those varieties bred for winter storage

| Turnips | 32 degrees F | 90 to 95% | Four to six months |

The above list gives you some idea of the temperatures and humidity levels that certain foods need to be stored at. The next chapter goes into more detail about foods you can store.

Chapter 3: What to Store in a Root Cellar

When deciding what to grow or purchase for storage in a root cellar, you need to consider a few things:

- What varieties you grow or buy
- If growing your own, your timing for each harvest
- The right conditions for storing each fruit and/or vegetable

All of this will ensure that your food supplies last as long as possible without spoiling and losing flavor or nutritional value. Typically, you will have some food that needs to be stored in damp, cold environments and others that need a drier and warmer environment. In the list below, the produce has been sorted according to their temperature requirements, providing information on how to harvest and store it, along with a few good storage varieties.

Cold and Damp

All the fruits and vegetables listed must be stored at 32 to 40 degrees Fahrenheit and 90 to 95 percent humidity.

Apples

Everyone you talk with will have their opinion on what apple varieties store the best, but the consensus is that heirloom and antique varieties do not store as well as newer ones. One exception is a variety called Winter Banana. It is also well-known that sweet apples don't store as well as the tart varieties.

How to Store

1. *Pick your apples* — Choose unbruised, unblemished, fully ripe fruit. Any cut or bruised apples will quickly go bad, meaning it can destroy an entire box of fruit. Try to ensure they have the stems on, as these will store for longer than those without.

2. *Protect your apples* — If your apples are being stored long term, they must not touch each other. Wrap each one individually in newspaper—if using recycled paper, ensure you know what ink has been used. Most newspaper print is soy-based, but some still have toxic chemicals and metals—not something you want your apples to be in contact with. Do not use glossy papers, such as magazines or newspaper inserts. These are usually printed with toxic ink and do not have the same protective qualities as conventional newspapers. You could also use paper towels, butcher paper, or paper bags. If you prefer not to wrap the apple, place

them in boxes with clean straw, damp, clean sand, or sawdust, ensuring the apples do not touch one another.

3. *Pack your apples* — Lay your apples in layers in a small/medium cardboard or wooden box. Be careful that you do not bruise them. Don't use large boxes as you need to check your apples regularly—too many apples in a box makes this hard.

Make sure you check your apples at least once a week for rot and use or dispose of any that look like they are going off.

Do not store near other fruits/vegetables because apples give off ethylene gas, which can cause other foods to overripen and spoil quickly.

Varieties

The following varieties are ideal for long-term storage:

- Arkansas black
- Criterion
- Cameo
- Honeycrisp
- Fuji
- Northern Spy
- Newtown Pippin
- Rome Beauty
- Pink Lady
- Yates
- Winter Banana

Shelf Life

Between two and seven months, depending on the variety.

Beets

Beets should be harvested once the weather has been dry for a few days, provided the roots have a diameter of around 2 inches. Dig the beets up, cut the greens off, making sure to leave 1 to 2 inches on the root, and brush off the loose soil.

Do not wash the beets. Simply store them in a lidded bucket or a wooden box filled with peat moss, sawdust, or damp sand. Make sure your beets do not touch each other. If you are using a bucket, put the lid on as this will help retain moisture, but do not tighten the lid (you still need air circulation).

Check on your beets every now and then and remove any that look like it is going bad—like apples, one bad beet can destroy the lot.

Varieties

The following varieties are ideal for long-term storage:
- Long Season
- Boltardy
- Lutz Green Leaf

Shelf Life

Beets will store anywhere between three and five months.

Broccoli

Broccoli is not well known for being a long-storage vegetable. That said, when stored correctly, you can make it last for a couple of weeks.

Dig up your broccoli and trim the stems. Now, you can store it in perforated plastic bags or hang it upside down in the cellar. However you do it, make sure you do not store it near any fruit, such as apples, that releases ethylene gas as this can dramatically shorten its storage life.

Varieties

The following varieties are ideal for long-term storage:
- Green Comet
- Greenbelt
- Marathon
- Legacy
- Waltham 29

Shelf Life

Between one and two weeks at most.

Brussels Sprouts

Love them or hate them, Brussels sprouts are good for storing—although they do not have a long shelf life. To get the best flavor from your sprouts, wait until several frosts have passed before harvesting. If your cellar is large enough, carefully dig the plant up and plant it in a container. Place it in your cellar and carry on harvesting it. Alternatively, hang it in the cellar by the roots. If you don't have much space, harvest your sprouts and store them in perforated plastic bags.

Varieties

The following varieties are ideal for long-term storage:

- Long Island Improved
- Jade Cross

Shelf Life

Between three and five weeks.

Cabbage

Red cabbage varieties will store better than their green or white counterparts, and late varieties are better than early ones.

Harvest your cabbages when the first frost has passed. Pull or dig the plant up and trim the leaves off. Choose cabbages with solid, unblemished heads to store.

These are best stored in bins or outside pits — if you store them indoors, the cabbage odor will go right through the cellar or house and can have a serious impact on how pears, apples, and celery taste. If you can only store them in the root cellar, each head should be wrapped in paper and stored on a shelf, with a few inches between each one.

Varieties

The following varieties are ideal for long-term storage:

- Danish Ballhead
- Brunswick
- Red Acre
- Late Flat Dutch
- Storage No 4
- Red Drumhead

Shelf Life

Between three and four months, depending on the variety.

Carrots

Carrots are one of the best root crops for storing right where you grew them in the garden — but only if you do not have any pest issues and can mulch the carrots with one to two feet of straw or hay.

If you need to store them inside, harvest them from the ground when the season is over before the ground freezes. Cut the tops off as close to the carrot as possible, leaving just a tiny bit, or snap them off. Leaving too much green will only deplete the carrot's nutrients and moisture, and they will not last long.

Lay the carrots in boxes filled with peat, moss, or damp sand.

Varieties

The following varieties are ideal for long-term storage:
- Danvers
- Kingston
- Chantenay
- Carson
- Bolero
- Nigel
- Kurota Chantenay
- Royal Chantenay
- Red Core Chantenay
- St Valery

Shelf Life
Between four and six months, depending on the variety and storage conditions.

Jerusalem Artichokes

Jerusalem artichokes store better in the ground than in root cellars, lasting the entire winter long as the ground does not freeze. If you opt to leave them in the ground, you must take precautions because exposure to frost and freezing conditions will break the starches down. Their texture, color, and flavors will change, and if any are diseased or bruised, they will spoil very quickly.

If you want to store them in your root cellar, dig them up, remove the tops, and brush off the soil. Store them in plastic bags or damp sand in containers. They must not be stored in areas where they can dry and shrivel up, as they do not store as well as potatoes do.

Varieties
The following varieties are ideal for long-term storage:
- Fuseau (most common)
- Coris Bolton Haynes (less common)

Shelf Life
All winter in the ground, provided the ground does not freeze. If stored in the root cellar, up to ten days in plastic bags and one to two months in sand.

Leeks

Leeks are another vegetable that can survive in the ground over the winter or until the first hard frost. Mulch your leeks heavily and keep them that way until after the frost. Dig them up, making sure their roots stay intact.
Fill a deep bucket with soil or damp sand and plant the leeks upright in it.

Varieties

The following varieties are ideal for long-term storage:

- Musselburgh
- Arena
- Elephant
- Nebraska
- Zermatt

Shelf Life

Between three and four months in the cellar, all winter in the ground, provided you do not get frost.

Parsnips

Like carrots, you can also leave parsnips growing in the ground over the winter. Cover them in heavy mulch and harvest them when needed. However, parsnips are not fond of freeze/thaw cycles; if your winters are cold, it is best to harvest them.
Lift them at the end of the season, before or just after the first frost, and cut off the tops. Store in boxes layered with sphagnum moss, damp sand, or peat.

Varieties

The following varieties are ideal for long-term storage:

- Hollow Crown
- All-America
- Offenham

Shelf Life

Between one and two months.

Pears

Pears are incredibly sensitive to changes in temperature and should be stored at the lower end of 29 to 31 degrees. If you store them at higher temperatures or for too long, the pears do not ripen. Instead, they break down, turning brown and mushy inside, while the outside still looks fine.

Like apples, you should store only the unbruised and unblemished fruits, preferably with their stems on. Each pear should be wrapped in a paper bag or newspaper and stored in wooden or cardboard boxes with a perforated plastic lining. This allows air circulation while keeping moisture levels up.

Varieties

The following varieties are ideal for long-term storage:

- D'anjou
- Comice
- Bosc

Shelf Life

Between two and three months.

Potatoes

Potatoes are one of the best root vegetables to store in a root cellar—unsurprisingly so, considering they were the original reason root cellars were built.

Wait until the foliage has died back, and then leave the potatoes in the ground for another two weeks. This helps cure the skin and harden it for storage. Dig up your potatoes carefully and sort through them.

Place any bruised or damaged potatoes to one side to be used straight away. If any have green spots, do not eat them—the green is a chemical that can cause digestive and intestinal upset.

Grade the potatoes by size—you want to store the same-sized potatoes together and brush off any dirt. Do not wash them. Now place the potatoes somewhere dark, at 45 to 60 degrees, for further curing for ten to fourteen days.

Once this is done, you can store the potatoes in bins, boxes, or burlap sacks. Boxes or bins should have shredded paper between each layer of potatoes and have air holes cut in the sides.

Do not store potatoes near any fruits that give off ethylene, and do not allow the temperature to rise as this will prompt the potatoes to start sprouting.

Varieties

Most late potato varieties will store just fine (early and second early varieties are not meant for storage). The following varieties are ideal for long-term storage:

- All Blue
- Red Pontiac
- Kennebec
- Sangre
- Katahdin
- Yukon Gold
- Sebago

Shelf Life

Between four and six months.

Rutabagas

Rutabagas, like most root vegetables, can stay in the ground over winter. You can add a ten- to 12-inch thick layer of mulch to stop the ground from freezing, extending it about 18 inches on either side of the row. Even if you get a couple of feet of snow, the roots are protected. However, they must all be harvested before the spring; otherwise, new growth will start from the tops.

If you cannot leave them in the ground all winter, lift them at the end of the growing season, brush the dirt off, and twist off the tops — this will ensure you can store them for longer. You should not wash them, but they must be 100 percent dry before you put them into storage if you do.

Sort through the roots and put aside any that are damaged — these cannot be stored and must be eaten straight away.

Layer the good roots in a wooden box or bucket with sawdust, peat moss, or damp sand. The roots should be packed and covered but not touching one another, and the container should not be completely sealed to allow the moist air to circulate.

Varieties

The following varieties are ideal for long-term storage:

- Laurentian
- American Purple Top

Shelf Life

Between two and six months, depending on the variety.

Turnips

These should be treated the same as carrots and kept moist. However, unlike carrots, turnips should be stored in an outdoor pit if possible. Otherwise, the smell permeates and taints the flavors of other foods.

Varieties

The following varieties are ideal for long-term storage:
- Purple White Top Globe
- Navet des Vertus Marteau

Shelf Life

Between four and six months.

Winter Radishes

Winter radishes can withstand temperatures down to 28 degrees outdoors and can be left in the ground, provided they are mulched heavily. However, should you need to store them out of the ground, consider an outdoor ground pit or garbage bins as they give off a very heavy odor indoors.

If you store them in a root cellar, cut the tops off, leave an inch of stem, and place them in boxes or baskets layered with sphagnum moss or sand.

Varieties

The following varieties are ideal for long-term storage:
- Chinese White
- Black Spanish
- Violet de Gournay

Shelf Life

Between two and three months.

Cool and Dry

The vegetables and fruits on this list should be stored at 50 to 60 degrees Fahrenheit at 60 to 70 percent humidity.

Dried Beans

Once your beans have grown and fruited, leave the pods on the plant until they are dry — the beans should rattle in the pods, indicating that they have dried. Then, dig up the plant and leave it somewhere shady and protected for another one to two weeks. To test if they are ready, press your thumbnail into the pods; if it leaves an indent, they need to be left to dry for longer.

The beans should be shelled by hand or beaten against a wall to drop out. Then, use a compressor or hair dryer to blow the chaff away and place the beans in an airtight container.

As beans are prone to weevils, you can freeze-dry them for a few weeks before storing them. For this, place them in single layers on trays in the freezer and leave for several weeks.

Varieties

The following varieties are ideal for long-term storage:
- Black Coco
- Adzuki
- Jacob's Cattle
- Brown Dutch
- Steuben
- Speckled Cranberry
- Yin Yang
- Repokeb (Tiger's Eye)

Shelf Life

Up to one year.

Garlic

Garlic is one of the easiest vegetables to store. First, wait until half of the leaves have begun dying, turning yellow or brown, yet still have green leaves at the top, and then dig up a bulb to check it. If the heads are loose but have not split, you can harvest them; if they are still tight, leave the rest a bit longer.

Dig the garlic up and brush off the loose soil. Be careful in your handling. Leave the garlic somewhere well ventilated to dry and cure, ensuring the bulbs cannot get sunburned or wet. Leave them for ten to fourteen days.

After this time, braid the leaves together, hang the garlic up, cut the tops off, and store the bulbs in a mesh bag. They must be kept in dry conditions; otherwise, they will begin sprouting and will not be nice to eat.

Varieties

The following varieties are ideal for long-term storage:
- Marbled Purple Stripe
- Chilean Silver
- Porcelain
- Mother of Pearl
- Tipatilla

Be aware that the hard neck varieties are not so easy to store as their soft neck counterparts.

Shelf Life

Between five and eight months.

Onions

Lift the onions when the tops turn brown and fall. Dig them up during a dry day and spread them on hardware cloth, a screen, or newspaper. Let them sit somewhere cool, dark, and well-ventilated for ten to fourteen days, or until the roots have dried and the skin has turned papery.

Cut the tops off, leaving about an inch, and store them in paper bags, net bags, or even pantyhose. Do not use plastic containers or bags that are not breathable — if onions are not stored in dry conditions, they will begin sprouting.

Varieties

The following varieties are ideal for long-term storage:
- Brunswick
- Australian Brown
- Copra
- Red Burgundy
- Bronze d'Amposta
- Newburg
- Red Creole
- Norstar
- Red Weathersfield
- Stuttgarter
- Rossa di Milano
- Yellow of Parma

- Yellow Globe

Sweet varieties do not store very well.

Shelf Life

Between five and eight months.

Pumpkins

Pumpkins should be harvested before the first frost; they do not like cold weather, and frost will kill them. Leave about an inch of stem on the pumpkin as this stops them from spoiling.

Leave them to cure for about ten days—the temperature should be 80 to 85 degrees. If your weather is warm and dry, you can leave them outside. The curing process hardens the skins, ensuring they store for longer. However, you should not store any that are bruised, damaged, or have broken stems.

The pumpkins can then be piled up in your root cellar, two or three deep, so long as they are in a dry area—off the floor may be best.

Varieties

The following varieties are ideal for long-term storage:

- Winter Luxury
- Howdens

Shelf Life

Between five and six months.

Squash

Squash is cured and stored in the same way as pumpkins, except for acorn squash, which does not need to be cured.

Varieties

The following varieties are ideal for long-term storage:

- Delicata
- Crown Prince
- Hubbard True Green Improved
- Golden Delicious Hubbard
- Waltham Butternut
- Uchiki Kuri

Shelf Life

Between four and six months.

Sweet Potatoes

Sweet potatoes should be harvested as soon as the vines have died back, usually in late fall. Dig the potatoes up carefully, putting any damaged tubers to one side for immediate consumption. Brush the loose soil from undamaged tubers and cure them for five to ten days, at a temperature of 80 to 85 degrees and 90 percent humidity.
After this time, you can move them into the root cellar, wrapping each tuber in paper and layering them in ventilated baskets or boxes.

Varieties

The following varieties are ideal for long-term storage:

- Centennial
- Allgold
- Jewell

Shelf Life

Between four and six months.

Tomatoes

You do not have to wait for your tomatoes to ripen on the vines. You can pick them still green and allow them to ripen while in storage or choose varieties better suited to longer storage. Provided the conditions are right, some tomatoes store much better than others. If you are storing green tomatoes, pull the whole vine from the ground and hang them in the cellar upside down. Alternatively, you can pick the tomatoes and wrap each one in paper. Store them at about 55 degrees so they ripen slowly — do not go below this temperature, or they will not ripen. At the ideal temperature, green tomatoes generally take ten to fourteen days to ripen.

Varieties

The following varieties are ideal for long-term storage:

- Eva Purple Ball
- Green Thumb
- Fried Green Hybrid
- Old Fashioned Garen Peach
- Reverend Morrow's Long Keeper
- Red Siberian

- Red October
- Winter Keeper
- Ruby Treasure

Shelf Life

Between one and two months for standard green tomatoes; up to six months for long storage varieties.

Chapter 4: Easy DIY Root Cellar Alternatives

Not everyone has the room to build a root cellar, but did you know that you do not need one? If you only have a small space at your disposal and don't grow vast amounts of produce but still want to store it, there are tons of ways to do it. Try some of these neat, easy, and cheap ideas:

Garbage Can Root Cellar

Materials:

- A metal garbage can with a lid
- A waterproof covering—a tarp or sheet of plastic
- A shovel
- Some straw

Garbage can root cellars are ideal for root vegetables such as carrots, potatoes, turnips, and parsnips. It is nothing more than a hole dug in the ground, the can buried, and your vegetables stored inside. Here is how to do it:

First, you need to choose your site. Trash can root cellars should be placed somewhere well-draining, so do not bury it where water can pool when it rains or runs off other parts of your garden.

Next, dig your hole. Evidently, your garbage can has to fit inside but ensure that the top of the can protrudes several inches from the soil.

Pop your root vegetables in and put the lid on.

Pile the straw on top of the can about one to one-and-a-half feet thick, ensuring all exposed parts of the garbage can are covered.

Lay your tarp or plastic sheet over the top; this ensures rain cannot get between the can and the lid and soak your vegetables. It also helps keep the straw in place.

Whenever you open the can to get vegetables out, check the others. If you spot any starting to rot, growing shoots, or beginning to shrivel, remove them and discard them. Leaving one rotten vegetable in there can destroy your entire storage.

If you do not intend to get vegetables out regularly, make sure you check the contents of the can at least once a week but never leave the lid off for long periods. Stored vegetables must not be exposed to the light for too long as it shortens their shelf life.

Bucket Root Cellar

Materials

- A five-gallon plastic bucket with a lid
- A drill
- A shovel
- Straw (optional)

Five-gallon buckets make the perfect miniature root cellar for onions, potatoes, and other root vegetables.

First, cut the bottom out of the bucket using a sharp knife or another cutting tool.

Next, dig a hole in the ground big enough to accommodate the bucket leaving its top flush with the soil line.

Fill the bucket with your vegetables and put the lid on.

If your vegetables need to be insulated from the cold, place a thick layer of straw over the top and, if necessary, cover with plastic to keep the rain out.

Although this holds fewer vegetables, you still need to check on them regularly to ensure none are going bad.

Freezer Root Cellar

Materials:

- An old chest/upright freezer or refrigerator
- PVC piping
- A shovel
- A tarp or large plastic sheet

If you are about to replace your freezer with a brand-new one, do not throw the old one out—you can easily repurpose it into a root cellar. However, you may need to get a specialist out to remove the freon gas if there is any left in the freezer.

If you don't have a freezer or refrigerator to repurpose, head to your nearest scrap yard and scour for one.

Remove all of the working parts from the freezer or refrigerator. Make sure you strip the back off and remove all mechanical parts—you should be left with nothing more than a shell.

Now, you need to make some holes in the back of the freezer. Use a drill with a small drill bit—this seems to work well. Do not worry if the drill breaks the plastic back; air holes are critical to the success of this project as they allow the air to flow into the root cellar. In the ground, provided you dig deep enough, the air will remain at a temperature of around 55 degrees Fahrenheit, which stops your vegetables from freezing over the winter.

Attach a layer of fine-meshed bug netting over the back, covering the holes. Although your freezer will be in the ground, you have no way of knowing what creepy crawlies are down there—and you don't want them anywhere near your vegetables.

Punch a hole in the top and the bottom of the freezer. Again, this is to aid in air circulation, helping air coming in through the holes on the back to circulate out to the surface. Proceed cautiously; do this right, and it will not draw in the cold air—sufficient circulation will see to that.

Insert pipes into both holes. How long these are will depend on the depth of your root cellar in the ground. Ideally, you should try to have them extending two to three feet out of the ground and attach vents to the top—this will stop dirt and water from falling down the pipes and into your root cellar.

Now you are ready to dig your hole, and how large depends on what size refrigerator or freezer you are using. Some people use a backhoe—it is a lot of digging—but you might not have access to one. If you have to dig yours by hand, take it easy—there is no rush! Line the bottom of your hole with bricks or rocks, making sure it is an even layer. This will help the air to flow better.

Carefully get your freezer or refrigerator into the ground, in its final resting place. Ensure you leave sufficient space to get the door open, especially if you are burying it near a building.

Fill in around the freezer with dirt but leave space around it. The easiest thing to do is place boards around the freezer a few inches out, making a box. This will stop dirt from being kicked into the freezer when you open it; it also makes it easier to put a heavy cover over the freezer later.

Now, while some regions have relatively mild winters, others have much colder and harsher ones. If yours is the latter, you will want to add some insulation over the top. This reduces the level of cold that can blow over the top, making it freeze.

Make your cover—this should be big enough to go over the top of the freezer and heavy. It will help stop your freezer from getting too cold and potentially freezing everything inside it.

You are now ready to fill your freezer with your vegetables. Layer them in, remembering to keep apples and other fruits that give off ethylene gas separate. Keeping the baskets in your freezer or refrigerator can help with this.

Remember, when you pull anything out of storage, you must check everything else to ensure it is not rotting or showing signs of spoiling.

Now, everything you do will have a learning curve, and this is one potential scenario. Say you fill your freezer with lots of fruits and vegetables, and everything is fine—until the temperatures plummet hard. Then, when you go to your cellar, you find that all your vegetables have frozen solid. Some can be salvaged, but all your squash and pumpkins are gone.

All you needed to do—and should have done from the beginning—was add a temperature sensor. A simple sensor plug will do, which switches a light on when the temperature falls below a certain level. A halogen bulb is sufficient—it will raise the temperature just enough to stop everything from freezing. That is your final step; adding your temperature sensor and bulb!

Pallet Root Cellar

Materials

- Six good-quality wooden pallets
- A tarp or thick plastic sheet
- A shovel
- Tools to cut the pallets

Pallets make a perfect underground cellar for root vegetables and dried goods. However, unless you can source your pallets for free, this might cost you a little.

Get your six pallets together—you can make it bigger or smaller as you wish. If you cannot find any, head to a garbage pick-up point, furniture movers, or builder's merchants—they usually have some on hand, but they may charge you for them.

Measure the pallets; standard ones are usually four feet by four feet.

Dig a hole a few inches bigger than the pallets, allowing sufficient space for the top pallet to be 6 inches beneath the ground. So, if your pallets are four feet square, dig the hole at least four feet in depth and width.

Use a tarp or a sheet of thick plastic to line your hole, making sure it is big enough to drape loosely in the hole.

Put the first pallet at the bottom of the hole—this is your floor—taking care not to tear or damage the plastic sheet.

Stand on the bottom pallet and place four more around to form the walls of your cellar. At this stage, because the pallets are all the same size, they will not support one another. Cut two bits of 4" x 2". They should be the same width as your pallets. Attach them to the end or side pallets—it does not matter which—using thick, strong string, or bailing twine/wire. This will stop your pallets from falling in.

Use string or wire to attach the pallets to each other at the corners, giving you a strong, sturdy box.

Standing inside the box, pull the plastic inside, and then fill the gap between the outer walls of your box and the sides with loose dirt.

Pack the dirt in, ensuring the box is firmly planted in the ground before getting out. Then walk around it, tamping the soil down, and remove the plastic from inside the box by rolling it up—you will need this for the next step.

You can now put your food into the box. Use thirty-gallon plastic bins to store your food, fill the box, and put the final pallet on top. Place the rolled plastic on top, keeping it cool inside.

You can add hinges to your top pallet if you want, and you can even make shelves to put in the box. After all, this is just a basic root cellar—you can make it as big or fancy as you like.

Once your cellar is full and the lid is on, add at least 3 inches of newspaper on top and pull the plastic back over the top. Cover it with a tarp and weigh the tarp down using bricks, ricks, or whatever else is at your disposal.

That is all you need to build a basic root cellar for your food. Pack the food in carefully, and you can store it for months. The only natural disaster this type of cellar cannot withstand is severe flooding. So, it is not best if your land is permanently soggy or if you live where there are high water table levels.

A Basement Cold Storage Room

Materials:

- Assorted pieces of wood
- Assorted tools
- Insulation
- Vents

If you have a reasonably sized basement and can afford the space, you can construct a cold storage room in one corner. This is not the easiest one to build. You will need to do plenty of research to learn how the air will circulate and manage humidity and temperature levels.

Simply select a corner in your basement, wall it off, and insulate it. The walls give you the cooling effect you need, and the insulation stops the cool air from circulating the rest of the basement. If you are not confident in doing this, hire a contractor specializing in this line of work to help you.

First, choose your corner. You need your room to have the best possible exposure to the exterior walls—the more concrete or stone there is, the better. Ideally, one wall will be exposed north.

Install a pair of dryer vents of approximately 4 inches. This will result in a kind of siphon, which allows you to regulate how the external air circulates the insulated room. If you can, get vents where the damper control is manual and with internal screens that stop insects and other pests from entering the room. They should be installed at least 10 inches away from one another and caulked in well.

Using PVC piping or dryer pipe, run some ductwork from one vent down to the floor—this will ensure the cold air goes downward. It flows through the vent, down the pipe to the floor, and the warm air will rise, exiting the second vent. Although it is optional, you can add a small exhaust fan to help with the airflow.

Build your wall and doorway frames.

Use 2-inch-thick extruded polystyrene boarding to add insulation to the interior walls. This type of boarding is resistant to moisture, relatively cheap, easy to work with, and works well with temperature changes in the evenings and at night.

Secure the board using polyurethane adhesive — construction quality is best — making sure to apply it in a continuous line.

The exterior walls will not be insulated as they do not need it, so don't make the mistake of thinking a double layer of insulation will help.

Add a vapor barrier on the warm side of the walls — plastic works best — and tap up the seams.

Use drywall or paneling to cover the external walls. However, do not put any finishing on the interior walls.

Use another vapor barrier to insulate the ceiling in your cold room, covered with rigid foam insulation.

Plan how your shelving will be arranged to allow the best air circulation — metal shelves mounted from the ceiling work well.

Lastly, install your door. It must be insulated and the base sealed with weather stripping. Now, you are ready to stock your cold room. Ensure you clean this room regularly as debris or dust building up can stimulate mold, which you don't want anywhere near your produce.

A Zeer Pot

Materials

- A large clay pot
- A small clay pot with a lid
- Duct tape
- Sand

Zeer pots are fascinating and fun to make. You can use these to keep food cool, and it works thanks to the water that evaporates from the combination of two different-sized pots and the sand. They are also very easy to make, so if you have kids, you can use this opportunity to teach them some science!

Get your supplies together, and make sure your clay pots are big enough to store the food you want. Alternatively, make several pots if you cannot find one big enough to start with. There are no size limitations — you can scale this up to any size you want, so long as the outer pot is a few inches bigger than the inner pot.

For example, if you want a Zeer pot with an outer dimension of 10 inches, you need:

- One clay pot, 8-inch diameter
- One clay pot, 10-inch diameter
- Insulation or soil
- Cotton or burlap
- A 12-inch potting tray
- Silicone, cork, or another type of watertight material for the plug

Start by putting the larger pot on a flat, stable surface. Once built, this will be quite heavy, so it is best to place it where you plan to use it. The best location has a steady flow of natural air, like a walkway between two buildings or on a balcony or terrace. You can even use a table next to an open window in a pinch, so long as there is a cross breeze. Place it on a large potting tray.

If your clay pot has a hole in the base, it must be plugged. Use a cork, duct tape, a rubber stopper, or anything else that will prevent leaking and is watertight. Cut your plug off so it is flush with the pot's base, and then seal it off using glue, duct tape, or wax. Ideally, you should get solid pots with no holes—that way, there are no chances of leaks.

Add a layer of soil, vermiculite, sand, or another insulating material to the bottom of the pot—it should be 1 to 2 inches thick. The depth will depend on your pot size, but the two pots must be even and level at the top rim, giving you space for the next step.

Place the smaller pot inside the bigger one in a central position and make sure the two tops are level. Looking at it from the top, you should see something that looks like the bulls-eye on a dartboard—an inner ring and an outer one with an even cavity between them.

Note:

If your smaller pot has a hole in the base, wrap the entire pot in plastic to create a waterproof barrier. However, be aware that this may slightly alter the evaporative and insulating properties.

You can now begin to add the rest of the insulating material. Pour it carefully in the space between the inner and outer pot. If you spill any into the inner pot, remove it before proceeding.

If you notice any water entering the inner pot at any time during these steps, you must start over, ensuring the inner pot is fully sealed. It must be dry and cool, and if water comes in from the bottom, this creates the perfect conditions for mold to grow.

Using a funnel, add your insulating material to the bigger pot, ensuring it packs in around the small one.

Now you are ready to begin adding water—do this slowly, allowing the material time to settle and add more insulation as needed. Once your material is saturated, place a layer of pebbles or small rocks on the top. These are not just to make it look nice. When you pour water over them, the stones ensure the material is evenly distributed and doesn't cut a channel through your insulation.

When it comes to the water you use, if you collect it from a pond, stream, lake, or river, you will need to filter it. Otherwise, you could end up contaminating your food since you do not know what may be in that water!

Check the pot for any leaks and use silicone to patch them. The potting tray will catch any water that leaks out and the surface your pot is on.

You can now put your food in. Don't be too hasty—the pots need time to cool before you start adding the food. If you are making the pot to stand in your garden, add the food a little at a time as it ripens until you are ready to start preserving it. Carrots and tomatoes will last for up to three weeks in a Zeer pot, giving you more time to harvest and potentially increasing your haul.

Once your food is in, the pit must be covered. There are a couple of ways you can do this. Place a lid on the inner pot; it could be a clay lid or an old glass slow cooker lid, so long as it fits the small pot snugly. Measure this before you start, as you may need to sand the pot a little to ensure a good fit.

Alternatively, take some cotton, cheesecloth, burlap, or another type of woven cloth big enough to cover the pot completely. Do not use polyester, blended materials, or any other synthetic material.

Soak the cloth in water and wring it out to remove the excess moisture. Lay the cloth over the pot and secure it (especially important if you experience high winds). Use twine, rope, an elastic band, or whatever you have on hand. Repeat to add more layers as needed, but be aware that air needs to flow up through the top—too much material will stop this. Conversely, more layers also stop pests from getting into your pot.

As the cloth dries, it will need to be changed for wet ones. If you used several layers, remove the top one, soak it again, and place it at the bottom of the pile. Rotating the cloth this way helps stop mildew and mold from developing because the layers are exposed to the air.

Monitor your Zeer pot and refill it as needed. To keep an eye on the water levels in the pot, you may place a piece of tube into the insulating layer. That way, you can see the water level inside and know when it needs topping up.

Cautions

While a Zeer pot is great for keeping food cool, it cannot substitute for a freezer. If you want to preserve frozen food, you can place it in a Zeer pot, where it will slowly defrost—much slower than leaving it out on your side.

These pots need two main things to be effective: moisture and airflow. If you don't have good airflow or it suddenly stops, your pot will not cool very well. In parallel, if you allow your clothes to dry out, evaporation won't be so effective. Also, consider the pot's location—whether there is any shade, the ambient temperatures, and humidity levels.

If you use your Zeer pot to store root vegetables or scallions, you could fill the inner pot halfway with damp sand. Your vegetables can then be buried in it, keeping it fresher for longer. With scallions, only the root part should be buried.

Things to note:

Eventually, your pot will accumulate a buildup of minerals. Dip a clean sponge in hot water or use some lemon juice to wipe this away from the pot's outer shell.

Breeze is required for the chilling effects. If you have a decent breeze or rig up a small fan, the pot will stay cold.

If external humidity levels are high, the pot won't be as efficient, so try to keep it in a ventilated, shaded area.

Lastly, be aware that a Zeer pot will go through at least two gallons of water per day in dry, warm, and breezy weather. Rather than wasting water when running a shower, collect the clean water and use this instead of running the tap. Alternatively, collect clean rainwater.

Build a Spring House

Materials:

- Assorted wood—2" x 4"
- Assorted tools
- A small stream or creek in your garden
- Cinder blocks
- A backhoe
- A shovel
- A measuring tape
- Hammer and nails
- Stone
- Cement
- Gravel
- Tin roof
- Windows
- A door
- Storm pipe
- A level

This method will only work if you have a source of fresh running water in your garden. Spring houses are a wonderful, traditional method of food storage, and the water ensures an even temperature throughout.

Your structure needs to be near a stream, creek, or another running water supply. The ideal location will have you build your spring house into the side of a hill with earth walls. If you cannot do that, make sure your location is level and beside the water. Try to avoid anywhere that is full of rocks and roots. The idea is to divert water from the spring, through the house, and back to the spring.

Measure the spring's depth in the center at several locations. You are looking for an average depth, so you know how deep to dig your trench through the house. Do not forget: Water will always find its level, so ensuring the trench is the average depth of the spring will enable the water to flow in and out of the structure easily.

Next, determine how long you want your spring house; this helps you work out where the spring will be diverted into and out of the building. The diversion point should be a few feet ahead of the walls.

Now, work out how far the distance is between the spring and the spring house. It should be close but not right next to it. If you dig your diversion trench too close to the spring walls, they are likely to collapse. Try to go for a width where you can walk safely between the spring and the house.

Time to decide on your structure. There are two ways to build a spring house: into a hillside or as a free-standing structure. Which one you choose will depend on your property layout. Building it into a hillside is deemed the most ecologically sound, using far fewer materials. However, there is always a trade-off—hillside houses take much longer to build than free-standing structures.

If you are building a hillside house, start by excavating the soil. Work out how wide and high you want the structure; it should be at least ten by ten feet and at least six feet tall to give you room to stand up. The entrance to your spring house should be on the opposite side of the diversion trench.

If you build a free-standing structure, you may use blocks, stone, bricks, or wood as per your preference. The most efficient method is to use a slip form construction with stone walls—it keeps the cost down because you can use materials around you. Blocks and bricks are also great choices if you are good at masonry, whereas wood constructions should be insulated to ensure the temperature is maintained.

Knowing how to build your spring house properly requires understanding how to get the floor right and why that matters. Once the walls have been determined, plan the spot where your structure will be built.

Start by digging a trench—it should be at least ten feet square and at least 6 inches deep. This depth will ensure the concrete does not crack when the ground contracts through seasonal changes.

The diversion trench should be built on the side near the spring, so dig a trench three feet wide, ensuring it is the average depth of the spring. Dig it from the side of the house to where it will return to the spring—at this stage, do not break through the spring bed.

Make your floor framework using 2" x 4" wood. You need two frames: a big rectangle and a narrow one. The big one frames the walkable space, while the smaller one frames the floor from the trench to the wall. The narrow rectangle should be the width of the wall as a minimum since one of the walls will rest on the concrete.

Place a 1-inch deep layer of gravel inside the frame and level it off. Fill the frame with concrete and level it off, removing air bubbles. The concrete will need a curing time of at least twenty-four hours.

While the concrete cures, decide if you want wood, stone, or concrete in the trench inside the house. Each has its pros and cons. While stone lasts longer, you need masonry skills. Wood is easy, but it rots quickly. Concrete lasts a long time, but you need to build a framework, and it needs time to settle and cure.

Use lumber to block the trench off and make the walls the required length for the water to flow through. Line the trench floor with a decent layer of gravel, eliminating the risks of any soil contaminants being picked up by the water.

The last thing to do is divert your water. You will need a covered trench for the entire length of the water coming in and flowing out of the house back to the spring. While the spring house will cover some of it, the inlet and outlet will not be covered.

Lay storm pipe in the trenches, ensuring enough to extend from the spring to interior walls, under the walls, and into your trench.

When the pipe is close to the spring, break through the bed and connect it so it extends into the spring. It must be at an angle that draws the water in and allows it to exit.

Check for leaks or weak spots in the pipe and, once you are happy, the storm pipe can be covered in soil. The entire line must be buried from the spring to the house, stopping the water from picking up contaminants.

Tips

Cinder blocks can be added at the trench sides inside the house. These should be half the trench height—tall items can stand in the middle of the trench, while smaller ones can go on the shelving at the side.

You can also build a wooden frame the same width but half the height of your trench—the length is down to your preference and need. The frame should fit snugly into the trench and be used to place storage items in so they do not get washed away.

The doors and windows should be in the north-facing wall; this allows sunlight to come in but stops direct sunlight from heating the room.

Finally, installing a tin roof will ensure a longer life span and keep heat out.

Make a Storage Clamp

Materials:

- Straw
- A shovel

This is one of the easiest ways to store vegetables and was originally used to store potatoes, carrots, and other root vegetables. Storage clamps are highly efficient and cheap to build; all you need to insulate the vegetables is soil and straw.

First, choose where your clamp will be. The ground must be level, well-draining—you do not want water pooling around your vegetables—and be sheltered from strong breezes and high winds.

Once you have determined your location, you can dig a pit. It should be about four feet in diameter and shallow.

Layer a 6-inch thick layer of straw in the pit and fluff it—this will trap the air.

Place your vegetables on the straw, making sure you only use unblemished and undamaged goods.

Add another layer of straw on top of the vegetables and around them—make it around 6 to 8 inches in depth.

Layer soil carefully over the top, again about 6 inches deep, leaving a bit of straw poking up—this allows ventilation in the clamp.

You can use a vegetable clamp to store vegetables for a few months. However, if the temperatures drop below freezing for a long time, you may find some of your crops will deteriorate.

You can bring your vegetables out through the straw on the top, but you may want to consider building several storage clamps to keep a mix of vegetables or one for each type.

An Outbuilding or Garage

If you do not want to build something and have another outbuilding on your property or in the corner of your garage, you can still create a root cellar.

However, these are only really good as seasonal cellars; even if you have insulation in the room, you will need to add more to ensure stable temperatures.

Garages are one of the best places because, typically, they are unheated, staying cool all year round. The most important things to consider are:

Ventilation

Your garage must have the correct ventilation — one of the most important factors in a root cellar. Regardless of the weather outside, you want to choose somewhere where the temperature remains stable.

The best ventilation is an airtight space. This ensures that your food stays fresh, but don't confuse airtight with little or no ventilation.

Proper ventilation stops mold from developing and accumulating. While these grow as mildew is trapped in the cellar, you can use simple pipes to ensure it is right in a garage. You need the air flowing into the garage and out of it—cool air must come in while stale, warm air must flow out. This helps remove ethylene gas from the space.

No Heat Insulators or Air Conditioning

Root cellars must withstand temperature variations, so it is unnecessary to add heat insulators or air conditioners to the garage. Plus, if you do that, you just bump up your electricity costs—and you do not need them in a root cellar anyway. Don't forget; root cellars have been around far longer than refrigerators or freezers!

Get the conditions in your garage right, and your food will stay fresh for weeks or even months.

Food Shelves

While ventilation is a key consideration, you also need to consider other things to keep your food fresh for as long as possible. One of those is making the best use of your space, as this will help your food last longer. Some foods are very sensitive to changes in temperature, so putting in a proper shelving system will help you get the right foods in the right places. Food that needs to be kept cool can go on the lower shelves, while foods that do well in warmer temperatures can go on the upper shelves.

Humidity

Provided you keep the humidity high in the garage, your food will not dry out. The humidity should be kept at around 80 to 95 percent, ensuring your fruits and vegetables retain their moisture. However, you must check on any food stored in lidded jars as these can rust due to the moisture in the air. Do not allow humidity to go above 95 percent, as that will destroy your fresh foods.

All in all, it is just a case of finding the right corner, putting up your shelves, optimizing your space, and going for it!

Container Root Cellar

If you can lay your hands on a large steel container, you can use it as a root cellar. All you need to do is bury it! However, before you go ahead and dig your hole, there are some things you need to consider:

1. **Zoning**

Before you can even think of using a steel container as a root cellar, you need to check if any zoning laws (city, county, or state) stop you from doing it or restrict where or how you do it. This will vary from region to region and may depend on what the ground is like and how far you intend to sink the container. You can choose to bury it completely, dig it into a hillside, or just bury it halfway. In any case, zoning laws may apply. First, run a quick search of your local and county websites and then start making calls — when a decision is made over the phone, ask them to confirm it to you in writing just to be on the safe side.

2. Placement

Chances are you already decided this when you checked out the zoning laws. When you decide this, think carefully about how you are going to use your container. If you build it into a hill, you will want a door and steps to access it. It is also worth noting that the deeper the container is buried, the more planning it will require.

3. Structure

If you choose to bury your container, you need to think carefully about how it will stand the pressure on it from the earth. Containers are not exactly designed to be buried; they were designed to be stacked on a ship or at the docks. The only load-bearing parts of a container are the four corner posts — the sides are strong enough to support the roof, and that is it. You may need to plan on erecting a retaining wall around where your container is located without forgetting to include drainage. If you do, heavy downpours could submerge your container, fully or partially. If you are completely burying your container, you will need a platform that pushes the earth's weight onto the four corner posts. The one thing you should never do is dig your hole and bury the container without planning — it will most certainly collapse.

4. Moisture

While containers are watertight and windproof, you need to consider how you will stop the earth's moisture from getting in. The floor is built of steel cross-members with treated plywood on top. You need to think about sealing underneath the floor and possibly pouring a cement base first. Your container also needs to be sealed with plastic tarps, roofing tar, or truck bed liners. Do your research and find the most cost-effective way of sealing your container for optimum results.

5. Ventilation

Your container cellar must have good ventilation and air circulation; otherwise, anything you store in it will be destroyed. The principle here is the same as any other type of root cellar.

Once your container root cellar is in place, you can follow the same rules for any type of root cellar. You can even add an extra door and use it as a storm shelter — at least it will have food in it!

Food Storage Shelves

If you have spare walls in your pantry or a spare room in your house, you can make a food storage system. Here, you can store fruit, some vegetables, and canned and dried foods—so long as your shelves are kept in a dark, cool place.
Later, you will read step-by-step instructions on building shelving units.

Crawlspace

If you have a crawlspace, you can certainly convert it, or part of it, into a storage room. Choose an area away from furnaces, water heaters, and other heat sources. Add sturdy shelving to give you more space; if it has a dirt floor, even better, as these are best at regulating humidity. Concrete floors are not ideal but will still provide a longer lifespan for most vegetables. Bring out your creative side without forgetting to include enough ventilation.

Plastic Tote

Plastic totes can easily be used to extend the life of your root crops. All you need to do is bury the vegetables partially in sawdust, which will help with moisture regulation and stop the vegetables from touching one another. Using a tote also means you can keep your vegetables in the dark. This method works well for potatoes, beets, and carrots, and you can also use straw if you cannot get sawdust—while it will need to be dried out, you can reuse sawdust or straw the following year.

Under Your Porch

If you are really clever and creative, you can use the space under your porch. One design is a hole in the basement wall leading to the under-porch space. Rigid foam is used to line it, adding insulation from external temperatures, and the entrance is designed to blend in with the room it came from.
These spaces are not huge but can be used to store several pounds of potatoes or other root vegetables in a space that would otherwise be unexploited.

Basement Window Well

If you have no extra space but have a basement window well, you can turn it into a miniature root cellar.

Ideally, your window well should be on a north wall. Cover it with orientated strand board (OSB) and a layer of straw bales. This keeps it cool but does not promote freezing. And if your window well is layered with gravel at the bottom, it will help regulate the humidity levels.

You can stack milk crates in there to hold your vegetables, and as these stack together well, you take full advantage of your space. You can also put dark curtains up at the window to keep the light out.

This type of storage works well for winter squash and potatoes. However, it is not ideal for those who are not very mobile, as accessing it can be quite challenging.

Earth Pit

This was another common method used to store root vegetables — this one is similar to clamp storage. All you need to do is dig a pit somewhere shady and well-drained, ensuring water can drain away and not into it.

Layer sawdust or sand over the bottom of the pit, add your root vegetables and cover them with more sawdust or sand and a thick layer of straw or leaves. Add a black plastic sheet and weigh it down using logs, rocks, bricks, or other heavy items.

Using Cardboard Boxes

If you have space in a room or even under your bed, you can use cardboard boxes to store your vegetables. The concept is simple: Place your vegetables in the box and cover them with something that will stay damp but not soaking wet. This makes your vegetables feel as though they are resting under the ground, just waiting to be picked. You can use any size cardboard box appropriate for the vegetables you want to store. The filling should be sand, peat moss, or wood chips for most vegetables (make sure your wood chips are not toxic) or newspaper for potatoes.

Most vegetables do not need to be washed before being stored — simply rub the dirt off potatoes, but most other things are fine being stored dirty. In fact, they should be, as the soil can help fight off diseases and protect the vegetables. The best way is to pick your vegetables or dig them up and place them straight in the boxes.

All root vegetables should be trimmed, leaving a couple of inches of top greenery on them to prevent them from deteriorating and drying out.

Potatoes

Lay some newspaper sheets in the bottom of the boxes.

Dig up your potatoes, sort out the ones for storage, and rub off the dirt. Be careful not to damage the skins.

Sort your potatoes by size or variety and place a single layer in the bottom of the box. Layer more newspaper and then add another layer of potatoes. Repeat until the box is full.

Other Root Vegetables

Spread a thin layer of filler material on the bottom of the box and add your vegetables. Try to lay them as per their shape—carrots are horizontal while turnips are upright. Add a layer of filler and then another layer of vegetables, and so on. Make sure the filler is moistened—this will act as a humidifier. Close the box and put it into storage.

Check on your vegetables regularly and remove any that are deteriorating or drying out. Beets are one of the worst for drying too quickly, but you can still use them if you get to them swiftly enough. Simply pop them into a pan of simmering water to revive them a little.

Provided you dry the filler out thoroughly, you can reuse it many times over.

Storing Vegetables in Sand

You can do this with just about any container you have on hand and a supply of fine sand (the type used in kids' sandboxes).

There are a couple of ways to go about this. First, you can use the crisper drawer in your refrigerator. Put a few inches of play sand in it and tuck in your root vegetables. You can also use this method for firm fruits like pears or apples. Cover with more sand, leaving a bit of space between the fruits/vegetables so they can breathe and the air circulate. You should leave about an inch between fruits.

Make sure you do not wash anything you store this way, as that will just hasten the decomposition process. Simply brush the dirt off and cut off green bits, like carrot tops or beet greens.

Another way is to add sand to wooden or cardboard boxes and store them in basements or cellars, even a garage—so long as it is not heated. It does not matter where as long as the temperature doesn't go below freezing.

The same procedure applies for the crisper drawer. Keep your fruits and vegetables separate, especially those that give off ethylene gas, such as apples. This gas speeds up the ripening process and can taint other vegetables and fruits. Store root vegetables vertically in the sand and the rest lying down.

In-Place Storage

There are a couple of methods for in-place storage; just pick which one suits you:

Garden Rows

Carrots and beets will store perfectly through the winter in this way, and in some cases, their taste may even sweeten over time.

The idea is to ensure the rows are insulated against sub-zero temperatures. You can do this by poking holes in a black garbage bag and filling it with wet leaves. Place it over the top and simply lift it off when you want to harvest your vegetables. Try to harvest enough to last you a couple of weeks so that you do not have to keep disturbing the rows, exposing them to the cold air. What is more, those leaves are perfect for adding to your compost heap when spring rolls around.

Another way is to cut the carrot tops off. Use the carrots—freeze, bottle, or whatever you want. The carrot tops can then be piled on another row of vegetables as insulation. After that, layer black plastic over the top and weigh it down with bricks.

Another method is mounding. Several pockets are dug into the earth and vented to allow the air to circulate. A drainage trench will ensure water is drained away from the pockets. The downside is that all the food in a pocket needs to be harvested at once, so it is best to create several small ones. The pockets are covered with straw and dirt layers to insulate them, and this method works for onions and potatoes, and any other food that requires storing in dry conditions.

Hay bale storage requires a structure made of hay bales to be built around your rows of vegetables. This is topped off with a large sheet of plexiglass or a recycled storm door, effectively turning it into a cold frame. A blanket or tarp can be used for extra insulation in very cold weather. This method allows you to harvest food as you need, not necessarily all at once, and works for crops that like moist conditions, such as carrots, winter radish, and beets.

The final method involves building mini hoop-houses over your rows. These are made from lengths of PVC piping and clear plastic sheeting. You can find many different ways of doing this online, they are pretty easy to construct, and they allow your crops to be harvested as you want them.

Chapter 5: Planning Essentials

Root cellars may well be considered a luxury nowadays, but back in the old days, they were as necessary as modern freezers and refrigerators.

If built properly, root cellars are a lifesaver, especially if you live somewhere remote, off-grid, or where power outages are common. Losing your refrigerator or freezer contents to a power cut can be devastating; a well-stocked root cellar means you will not starve.

With a root cellar, you can also bring your utility bills down. You can store as much in a decent root cellar as you do in a big walk-in refrigerator without the power bills that go with it!

And root cellars do not just give you a place to store your food; they can also provide shelter from adverse weather conditions.

So, as you know, a root cellar is a space that uses the earth's natural humidifying, cooling, and insulating properties to help preserve food. That said, for a root cellar to work, it needs three things: stable temperatures of 32 to 40 degrees Fahrenheit, ventilation, and 85 to 95 percent humidity.

You need stable temperatures to stop microorganisms growing on your food and to slow down how fast ethylene gas is released. Both of these will aid in the decomposition process, destroying your food stores.

The humidity stops vegetables, roots, and tubers from drying out and shriveling up.

Part of the planning process requires deciding what type of root cellar you want. Most people will try to dig a root cellar beside their house, alongside the foundations, thinking they will already have one wall for their cellar made from cement. However, this has one big problem—doing this runs the risk of undermining your house foundations, all for the sake of building something that could cost you little to nothing.

The ideal distance is around twenty feet, at the very least, from your house. Not only will you avoid upsetting your house foundations, but you can also avoid running into any issues with groundwater.

One of the best types of root cellars is the hillside option, where the root cellar is dug into a hillside, and the floor sloped toward the cellar opening to aid drainage. Sure, you can add drainage pipes to help keep your root cellar dry. However, bear in mind that, in the old days, people did not have PVC piping and drain pipes—they kept their root cellars dry by designing and building them properly.

If you opt for a pit-style cellar, the pit should be square and sloped at one end, allowing you to add steps over the slope.

Now, if you opt for the garbage can, make sure your can has holes in it—metal cans cannot breathe, and if you omit the holes, your food will spoil quickly.

Basic Tips

All households are different in their eating habits, and the design and contents of all root cellars will be wildly different depending on the household's needs. For most people, root cellars offer a great place to store root vegetables and tubers, such as carrots, potatoes, parsnips, beets, and so on.

You might ask why you cannot just go and buy these as you need them. Well, you can if you want; however, take a careful look at the quality of the vegetables in your grocery store. They are often damaged, bruised; some are already going off and are generally tasteless. If you have the room to grow your own or have a farmer's market nearby, a root cellar is the way to go—and face it, homegrown vegetables always taste better and more satisfying than store-bought.

You also have the added benefit of knowing that your food has not been sprayed with chemicals, pesticides, and whatnot. Besides, when the shelves are stripped bare and food shortages loom, you know you will not starve in times like the current pandemic—if it ever comes down to that.

As such, these are the basic principles that you need to follow in planning and building your root cellar successfully.

- **Check with your building department** — The last thing you need is to fall foul of any building regulations. Your local building department can tell you any requirements or regulations you must comply with before you begin constructing your root cellar. You must follow all construction or building codes that apply to your construction and ensure you have the permits you need—if applicable before you begin.
- **Draw up a plan** — Design your root cellar to meet your food storage goals and consider any physical disabilities you may have. For example, if you struggle to use a ladder or stairs, opt for a more accessible root cellar design.
- **Choose your size** — Your root cellar must be big enough to store all the food you want in there. For example, if you grow an acre's worth of food, it is no good building a tiny root cellar that will barely hold a fraction of what you harvest. Conversely, do not build a massive one if you only have a small amount to store. If you choose to build underground, bear in mind some precautions for building in enclosed spaces. Some potential risks include structural failure, unwanted gases building up, cave-ins, and so on. The last thing you want is to build a death trap by accident! Remember that immense weight is pressing down when you build anything underground, not just from the top but also from the sides. That is why it is critical to get your design and build right. So, design your cellar from the ground up, ensuring it is safe, sound, and has adequate ventilation.
- **Think about the location** — You must consider every aspect of the land where you want your root cellar. Some places have very high water tables, and some have septic systems—both of these can be catastrophic as the root cellar will flood and

fail. Also, consider how far away from your house the cellar will be. If you locate it a long way off, it will not be very convenient to keep going down there for some vegetables for dinner; it needs to be close and accessible. Some people have even constructed their root cellars beneath a garden shed, with access inside the shed. When it snows heavily in the winter, they can still access the storage without shoveling snow away first.

You also don't want to build in rocky soil or where there are tree roots. Not only do you need to chop through these, but they will start to grow again, which can compromise your cellar.

- **Factor in the important aspects** — When drawing your design, factor in controlling temperature, drainage, ventilation, and humidity. All of these are important and will affect how long your food will last in storage. Commonly, people approach building a root cellar based on what food they are storing. So, when you draw your plan, ask yourself these questions:
- Does my food need to be stored in a warm and dry environment, a moist and cool environment, or a dry and cool environment?
- Does my food require ventilation to remove excess ethylene gas, saving my food from rotting or starting to sprout?

Perhaps the best way to design your root cellar is with flexibility and the option to control its climate as per your storage needs. After all, you may not grow the same things every year.

- **The foundations** — Next, you need to plan your cellar's foundations. You will need to dig a minimum of ten feet down—this will take you to the ground level, where the temperature stabilizes. If your soil is loamy or sandy, you might need to dig a bit deeper.
- **Lining the walls** — Use cinder blocks if you can—they are cheaper, more malleable, and excellent for lining your walls. Do not forget that your walls must be built on the foundation to ensure they stay up; you might be surprised at the number of people who put the floor in and then build their walls to the sides!
- **Plan your floor** — Many people think that pouring a cement floor is the best way to go, but in reality, the best flooring for a root cellar is gravel and natural dirt. This works to retain moisture better than a concrete floor. The idea is to keep humidity high; the more moisture you can keep in, the better.
- **What about the roof?** — Graded ceilings are far better for keeping the rain out, along with other external elements, and stopping them from resting on the cellar roof. Heavy rain or snow piled on the roof can add a lot of extra weight, all bearing down on your cellar foundations.
- **Ventilation** — This is a critical step in constructing your root cellar, as ventilation will stop too much humidity and moisture from spoiling your crops. Excessive moisture forms condensation, which, as you well know, means you will have water running everywhere, causing your crops to rot and spoil.

If you decide you want to convert an existing building or space, ensure you follow the same guidelines for location and make the right alterations to fit what you want.

Maintaining Your Root Cellar

While root cellars are relatively easy to maintain, you need to be on top of monitoring it, especially when yours is newly built at the start of the season. Two of the most important things you can invest in are a hygrometer and a thermometer. As established, you must maintain the following conditions in your cellar:

- Humidity — 90 to 95 percent
- Temperature — 32 to 40 degrees Fahrenheit
- Ventilation — Constant and properly installed

Keeping the temperature stable is possibly the hardest thing to do. Most root cellars rely on the soil temperature to keep the cellar cool. Based on your climate, you may need to consider digging your cellar in a bit deeper—this is why research is critical.

It is fairly simple to raise humidity levels—just leave a few water bowls in the cellar. Then, do some experimentation with humidity and see how many bowls you need to use to get the humidity at the right level. However, be mindful of ensuring your root cellar is secured—water can attract insects and other unwelcome creatures.

By contrast, if you need to lower the humidity level, make your ventilation a bit bigger or angle it to where the winds prevail from in your region. Make sure your ventilation is covered with a screen; otherwise, you will get insects, dirt, rain, and all sorts in your cellar.

Adequate ventilation will stop ethylene gas from building up and destroying your food or causing it to sprout too early. Ethylene is odorless and is typically associated with fruits like bananas and apples.

Ventilation Methods

All root cellars are different and will require their own methods for regulating ventilation and humidity. The critical thing to monitor is the conditions inside your root cellar and ensure you can alter your design if needed, preferably before you start building. Alternatively, ensure your design allows for alterations to be made at a later date. Perhaps the easiest way to vent your cellar is with two vents, about three to 4 inches wide. The first should be located near the top of the room and the second near the bottom to ensure optimum air circulation.

Lastly, you need to consider the lighting in your cellar. Essentially, a root cellar should be as dark as possible — too much light can lead to rotting and sprouting. By all means, have a single light bulb in your cellar but do not leave it on any longer than necessary. You can also cover your fruits and vegetables with burlap to keep the light out while allowing sufficient air circulation and ventilation. If you are using a window as your ventilation, cover it with dark material.

Organizing Your Space

How you design your space mainly depends on what you are storing. If you are only keeping one type of produce, ensure the humidity and temperature levels are even throughout the cellar.

Build shelves for the walls and other storage units using wood — they will not conduct the heat or cold the same way metal does and ensure the temperatures remain steady. Also, make sure your storage options are a couple of inches away from the walls to keep them dry. Using shelving means storing foods that need different temperatures, too — colder at the bottom, warmer at the top.

Lastly, load in your produce, and don't forget to check it weekly. Discard anything going bad and reap the rewards of all your hard work.

In the next chapter, you will be walked through building a simple, beginner-friendly underground root cellar.

Chapter 6: How to Build a Simple Root Cellar

Your garden is overflowing with fruit and vegetables, and while you can give some away to your friends, family, and neighbors, that still leaves you a ton of it. So, since you can only eat so much, what will you do with the rest?

You could spend days and inflate your electric bill canning some of it. You could shove it in your freezer, but what do you do when you run out of space? Plus, not all fruits and vegetables fare very well in the freezer or canned. So, the best answer is to build a root cellar.

There are plenty of options, and many have been covered in a previous chapter. Here, you will be walked through building an underground root cellar and a barrel-in-the-ground cellar, step by step.

Building an in-Ground Root Cellar

Building an underground root cellar requires time and commitment — in abundance — so if you do not have either of these, you will need to consider another type of root cellar. If you are not handy at building or don't have the right equipment, consider hiring an expert contractor to help you.

First and foremost, you need to choose the materials you will build your root cellar from. Some options include:

- Natural stone
- Cinder/concrete block
- Cedar logs
- Tires packed with dirt

Most people tend to choose cinder blocks as these are inexpensive and easy to come by in most builder's yards or DIY stores.

If you want to go down a different route and let your creative side have free rein, you could consider using a water tank made of fiberglass. These can easily be modified to your requirements and are easier to bury than digging out an entire room and building walls. Just make sure it is ventilated and has at least one foot of soil covering it.

For the in-ground root cellar, you will also need to consider your flooring. Most people use concrete, flat stones or leave it as a packed earth floor with a layer of gravel. That is the cheapest option and is often the best, as it ensures humidity can be better controlled.

Step One

Consider the location of your root cellar. It must be in an area that has well-draining soil—the last thing you want is water running in. You must also consider the water table—you cannot build an in-ground root cellar where the water table is high. Lastly, ensure that the opening is on a north-facing side—this limits the exposure to the hot sun during the day. Remember that you will need to factor in ventilation, temperature, and humidity wherever your root cellar is located.

Step Two

Dig that hole!

Depending on how large your root cellar is, you may need to use a backhoe or hire a contractor who has one to help you dig it.

Step Three

Dig down further for the footings all around the cellar and pour in the concrete. Now, you will need to leave this for at least twenty-four to forty-eight hours to harden.

Step Four

When the concrete has hardened off, you can begin building your walls. Take your time with this step—it is a substantial job, and trying to lay all the bricks in one go will result in disaster. Again, if you are not a confident bricklayer, consider hiring someone to do it for you.

At this stage, you should also ensure your ventilation is added. You want a PVC pipe, approximately 3 to 4 inches in diameter, inserted at the bottom of the cellar, drawing in the colder air. A second one, of the same size, needs to be installed near the top to vent the hot air and ethylene gas. Ensure your vent pipes have breathable screens over them—the air can still flow while keeping pests out.

As you are building the wall, frame your entrance. After all, you need a way to get in! Build the footings five brick rows high where the door will be.

Step Five

Make your roof. You could just pour a flat slab of concrete for the top, but you would have serious trouble with condensation. So, the best option is to build an arched roof. This requires great carpentry skills (or someone to do the job for you!).

You will need ½-inch plywood and 2x4s to build a strong enough structure; it will need to be built, taken apart, and reassembled on your cellar walls.

First, build your skeleton using 2x4s and plywood as shown below:

Next, use plywood to cover the roof of your structure.

Reassemble it on the cellar walls.

Place the plywood cover on top, cover it in a tight plastic sheet, and affix it to the structure before covering the entire roof with rebar.

Now, pour your concrete. It should cover the entire structure and the wall bricks and be around 6 inches thick. You will probably need to do this in sections unless you have a contractor helping you.

Now comes the time for patience! That concrete needs to be cured and dried before you can remove the wooden form from the inside. Leave it at least two to three days before you attempt to remove the form. You should also brush a waterproof sealant over the concrete.

Step Six

The next step involves building your stairs. This is best done with concrete—although you can construct wooden ones if you wish. Add a door at the top, one at the bottom, and your root cellar is ready.

Two doors are recommended because they help keep creatures out of your root cellar and the cooler air in—just make sure to shut the top door before opening the bottom one. You will also want a light of some sort atop the stairs so that you can see your way down.

If you have chosen to keep your cellar floor as packed earth, you can also layer gravel over it.

Organize your Cellar

Use wooden shelves on your walls; these are not so fast to conduct heat and cold and help you regulate your temperatures. All that is left to do is install a hygrometer and thermometer and start stacking your food in.

Building a Barrel Root Cellar

This is a much simpler way of building a root cellar, and this book provides the plans for two different types—a small and a larger one. First, the small one:

Materials

- A five-gallon barrel or trash can
- A drill and drill bit
- A shovel
- A hay bale

Step One

Determine where your barrel is going to be located. It should be somewhere shady and north-facing, as this will help keep your vegetables cool with minimum light exposure. If you have natural hills in your ground, use them, or you could pile soil up about six feet; these make perfect locations for barrel root cellars. If not, you can dig your barrel in—do be careful that you will not fall foul of water issues in the ground.

Step Two

Gather your supplies. You can use plastic buckets, metal trash cans, or anything that suits your needs, so long as it has a sealable lid.

Step Three

Get drilling. The earth is what regulates the humidity in a root cellar, and air circulation is a must. Drill some holes into the bottom of the barrel. You could cut off the entire bottom; either way, it will work.

Step Four

Dig the hole. This is straightforward—just make sure the hole is large enough for the barrel. Keep checking the size against your barrel and, when it is the right size, pop the barrel in for good. Fill in the edges using the earth you dug out and ensure that the barrel protrudes a couple of inches out of the ground.

Step Five

Fill it up. Pop your vegetables in, ensuring you do not mix vegetables and fruits that are not happy together. It may be best to build separate ones for each type of produce—that way, you eliminate the issue of ethylene gas. Do not wash your vegetables before you put them in as this can draw moisture out of them; simply dig them up, brush off loose soil, and put them in.

Step Six

Seal it up. Put your lid on, ensuring it seals tightly, and put a thick layer of hay or straw over the top. You can simply put a whole bale on to prevent your vegetables from freezing.

50-gallon Barrel Root Cellar

This is just a larger version of the previous design, which you can do in two ways depending on what you are storing.

Materials

- A large wooden barrel or a steel drum
- Sawdust
- Burlap sack
- Straw or piles of dead leaves
- Rocks
- Wooden leaves

If you only have apples to store, you can use the first method below.

Step One

Dig a hole in the ground, about half the depth of the barrel or drum — you only want it buried halfway into the soil. Put the barrel in and pack the earth around it.

Step Two

If you are using a steel or metal drum, you will need a layer of sawdust at the bottom and between the fruit and the sides of the barrel — freezing metal will quickly destroy your harvest.

Step Three

Fill the barrel with your apples. Cover the barrel with a burlap sack filled with dead leaves or straw and then heap soil up around the exposed sides of the barrel, leaving just the sack visible.

Step Four

Around the barrel, dig a drainage ditch. It should be about 6 inches deep and run around the outside of the heaped soil. Place some rocks on top of the bag to hold it down.

When you want apples from the barrel, simply remove the bag and take what you want. Be sure to watch out for any fruit going bad and discard it immediately.

For other vegetables

You can also use your barrel to store other vegetables besides apples, but the method is slightly different.

Step One

Ensure your barrel is going in a well-drained space and dig a hole. The barrel will be laid on its side and tilted down into the earth. This will ensure that any moisture can run out of the barrel.

Step Two

Layer the hole with dead leaves or straw to provide insulation, and lay the barrel in the hole. Place a piece of board over the bottom end to stop your vegetables from falling out. Then, pack the soil behind it to hold the board there.

Step Three

Cover the top end of the barrel and the sides with soil. The top end and side should be covered in about 18 inches of soil, tapering down to 3 inches at the lower end, up to the board.

Step Four

Cover the whole barrel with a thick layer of straw and top it off with heavy boards to stop the straw from being blown by the wind. You can do this in two ways; lay the boards on top, or construct a roof-like structure over the top, buried in the earth on either side.

The three types of root cellars have been covered here, and a previous chapter gave you many more ideas. Ultimately, you are bound to find a design that will suit your budget, space, and storage requirements, however big or small.

Chapter 7: DIY Shelving Systems for Produce

Once your root cellar is built and you are happy with it, the next step is to put in some storage options. Sure, you could just pile your vegetables in, but that would be a recipe for disaster. As you have seen, not all fruits and vegetables go together well, and some definitely should not be stored near others. Some require colder temperatures, while others like it a bit warmer. This chapter looks at ways to organize your root cellar, but first, you need some ideas on building easy DIY storage shelving. Here are three different ideas — feel free to adapt them to your requirements.

Slide-Out Shelving Racks

With a slide-out shelving rack, you can easily store and access your fruits and vegetables as you need them. These also make great racks for curing produce like potatoes or apples or ripening pears before putting them into storage for the winter. This easy slide-out rack also solves the problem of not having enough floor space to store everything you want.

Materials

- Four pieces of 2 x 2 wood, eight feet long
- Fourteen pieces of 1 x 3 wood, eight feet long
- Seven pieces of 1 x 2 wood, eight feet long
- Brad nails – 1 ¼-inch and 2-inch
- Self-tappet screws – 2-inch
- PH screws (pocket-hole screws) – 2 ½-inch

The first step is to cut your wood to the desired lengths. This will make it much easier for you to put it all together — you will not have to keep stopping to cut a bit here and there. Cut the following pieces of wood:

For the Vegetable Rack Frame:

- Legs — 4 pieces of 2 x 2, 41 ½ inches long
- Slide Drawer Gliders
- — 16 pieces of 1 x 3, 23 ½ inches long
- 2 pieces of 2 x 2, 41 inches long. Cut both ends at 60 degrees off square, keeping the ends parallel.
- 4 pieces of 2 x 2, 41 inches long. At the longest points, cut one end at 60 degrees off square and the other end at 30 degrees off square. Cut the ends in the same direction, making sure they are not parallel.
- Front and Back Supports — 4 pieces of 1 x 3, 25 ¼ inches long

For the Drawers

- 14 pieces of 1 x 2, 23 ½ inches long
- 14 pieces of 2 x 2, 20 ½ inches long
- 49 pieces of 1 x 3, 23 ½ inches long

Make sure to keep the pieces for the frame and drawers separate—you do not want to get them muddled up, or else it will make the job much harder!

Tools

Get all your tools together before you start:

- Good tape measure
- A speed square
- Pencils
- Safety glasses
- Ear protection
- A drill
- A circular saw
- A brad nailer
- A sander
- Stainer and brush

How to Make Your Vegetable Rack

Read through the following tips to make sure you understand all that is required.

First and foremost, ensure that you take all the right safety precautions and wear protective clothing/goggles/gloves where needed.

Ensure you are working on clean surfaces that are level, not chipped or cut, and have no other debris or imperfections. Make sure your boards are straight when you buy them—bent or twisted wood is not easy to work with, and the result will be less than desirable.

After every step, check that your build is square. If you don't and the finished project is not square, it will be a tough job to go back and find out where it went wrong.

Predrill your holes before you put screws in. This makes it easier to get the screws in, and you are less likely to split or damage the wood.

Your finished nails should be put in with glue, which provides a much stronger hold. If you intend to stain your vegetable rack, make sure to wipe off any excess glue—dried glue makes it hard for the stain to take.

Lastly, be safe and have a lot of fun with this project! Do not forget: If you don't know how to do something, get someone to help you who does—it may cost you a few dollars, but it will be much safer and more rewarding in the end.

Instructions

Step One

Starting at the top, work downward, attaching your 23 ½-inch pieces of wood to the two pieces of 4-inch long wood you cut for the frame. The pieces must be dead even on either side and be spaced at 2 ½ inches between them. That will make it 5 inches between the top of one piece of wood and the next. When you measure your diagonals from top to bottom (opposite corners), they should both measure 47 ¾ inches exactly. That way, you will know your build is square.

One important thing to ensure is that the ends are square and identical. Your side rails will work as drawer guides, so these must attached square. Otherwise, the drawers will not work. The side rails can be attached using glue and 2-inch brad nails.

Step Two

Now, you want to add your cross-braces — the two pieces of 41-inch 2 x 2 wood. These will add great strength to the rack and hold it square, so attach them diagonally to the back of the rack. You do not have to use both — one will do unless you opted to build a much bigger rack, in which case you will need both. Attach these from the inside of the rack, using glue and 1 ¼-inch brad nails.

If you use both, your center angles should be 30 degrees off square, and you should use PH screws to join them in the center.

Step Three

Add your front and back supports using the 25 ¼-inch pieces of wood, affixing them using glue and 2-inch screws.

Step Four

Time to build your trays — these must be completely square, or they will not slide correctly. Trays are built using 23 ¼-inch wood for the fronts and 20 ½-inch wood for the sides. Leave a ¾-inch gap between your slats (23 ¼-inch) to allow for good airflow. Check your diagonals — they should measure exactly 32 ¼ inches.

Build the first one and ensure it slides properly before you build the rest.

Step Five

Put your trays in, and your rack is complete! At least the build is. Now it is time to finish it off. First, add a little candle wax to the drawer slides and the drawer bottoms to ensure a smooth glide.

Go over the rack, filling all the screw and nail holes with wood filler, and then leave it to dry. Apply more as needed. When the filler has dried completely, you can sand your wood using 120-grit sandpaper, making sure to follow the wood grain direction. Next, vacuum it down to get rid of the mess and wipe it over with a damp, clean cloth.

If you are going to stain the wood, do it now and leave it to dry.

Fill it, and enjoy!

Multi-Purpose Flexible Storage

If you have gone to the trouble of building a fantastic root cellar, you do not want to spoil it—and your haul—by using second-rate storage shelves. By keeping in mind that your harvest is likely to be unpredictable from one year to the next and that you may have different produce each year, you can build flexibility into your storage. This flexible storage project includes bins, drawers, and shelves, all ventilated to allow airflow for all sorts of vegetables and fruits. This build is also fully customizable to your needs.

Materials

These quantities are for the basic build. If you want to customize it to your requirements, scale the materials up or down as needed.

- ¾-inch plywood in 4 x 8 sheets
- 1 x 2s pinewood
- 1 x 3s pinewood
- ½-inch plywood
- 1 x 10s pinewood
- Wood glue
- L brackets
- ¼-inch drywall screws
- 3d and 6d finish nails

Instructions

Step One

Cut the large sheet of plywood into strips—the length is based on how high your root cellar is, and the width should be 16 inches. Each shelf upright will require two strips. Spread wood glue on one strip's face and then apply the other strip on top. Use drywall screws to secure them together.

Step Two

Make a story stick*—this will help you ensure all the cleats on your shelf uprights are equally spaced. These will hold your shelves and should be 1 ½-inch wide, with a 1 ¾-inch wide space between them, allowing room for the shelves and bins to slide out. The top of the story stick should be held flush to the top of an upright, and the tick marks transferred to the edges of the panels. Using a framing or drywall square, extend the marks across the entire width of the panel. The story stick should be used on both sides to ensure your spacing is uniform throughout, and the uprights should all be marked in the same way.

(*A story stick is one of the simplest yet most valuable tools you can use when designing complex projects from wood. It is a rod or board used for checking the measurements that are repeated throughout the project. Graduated marks are made on the stick with a pencil, related to the specific project, and then used to ensure your measurements are correct. Using a pencil to make the marks, you can use your stick repeatedly for all your woodwork projects. How convenient!)

Step Three

Cut the 1 x 2 wood in cleats of 16 inches. Install them to the upright faces using drywall screws and glue. It is a good idea to drill pilot holes before putting the screws in — this stops your wood from splitting.

Step Four

Use L brackets, concrete anchors (if needed), and screws to attach your uprights to the walls, floor, and ceiling in your root cellar. Each pair should have a gap of 24 to 28 inches between them.

The spacing between the uprights determines the bin, drawer, and shelf dimensions.

Step Five

First, find or make a spacer to use as your spacing guide. It should be the same thickness as the spacing between your slats — 16d nails tend to work well.

Make your ventilated shelves. The 1 x 3 side supports and slats should be cut to length to fit your gap — although the slats should be ¼-inch shorter than the space you left between your uprights.

The slats should be positioned on top of the side supports, about ⅛-inch apart, to ensure sufficient air circulation. Ensure your slats are square to the supports by using a framing square. Use wood glue and 3d finish nails to assemble the slats on the supports.

Step Six

Now you can build the drawers. Cut plywood bases from ½-inch plywood to fit the gap between the uprights, ensuring the width is ¼-inch narrower. Cut some oval finger grips along the front — this is best done with a 1-inch spade bit in your drill and a jigsaw, allowing you to create the straight edges.

Build the drawer box from 1 x 4, making it narrow enough that the plywood will go 1 ½ inches beyond the front and sides. Assemble the frame using screws and glue.

Now spread glue on the base of the frame and put the plywood base on top — use 6d finish nails to secure it to the drawer box.

Step Seven

To build your bins, use 1 x 10 wood for the sides, and cut it so that the top edge is 19 inches long and the bottom edge is 15 inches long. Cut 16-inch runners from 2 x 2 and use glue and screws to secure them to the sides at the top. Cut slats from 1 x 3, 3 ½ inches shorter than the gap between your uprights.

Turn your side pieces upside down and install the slats on the back, front, and bottom using screws and glue. Use a spacer to ensure your gaps are even.

Put it all together, and you have one of the most versatile and flexible storage units, ideal for all sorts of produce!

2 x 4 Basic Shelving

One of the first things you should do when you organize a root cellar is get everything off the floor. The best way to do that is with a good set of shelves. Sure, they may end up cluttered with stuff, but you will soon sort it out and get everything in order.

Rather than making shelves, you could just go and buy some—there is nothing wrong with that. However, some people feel they have put so much work into building their root cellar that store-bought shelves just would not do it justice. And, to be fair, homemade shelving is more cost-effective. As an example, you could pay upwards of $80 to $100 for a 48-inch by 24-inch by 72-inch unit, while you could build one at least twice that size for the same price—and it will probably be assembled in less time!

Materials

- Thirteen 2 x 4s, 8 feet long (It might be wiser to get a couple extra, just in case something goes wrong.)
- Two sheets of 23/32 OSB subfloor, 4 x 8 (If you cannot get this, use plywood.)
- 3-inch screws—try not to use drywall screws
- A saw

Instructions

Step One

The first step is to do your measuring and cutting. The OSB sheets should be cut in half lengthwise, giving you four shelves of 2 x 8. There are a few reasons why you might want to consider having the store cut them for you:

1. It may fit easier in or on your car
2. It is far easier to unload and get to your root cellar
3. Less sawdust

Now for the corner posts. Cut your 2 x 4s to six feet. Cut one into four pieces 21-inches long for your end pieces, and use the 2-foot cut-offs from your posts to make a further four pieces 21 inches long.

In the end, you should have eight 2 x 4s, eight 21-inch long pieces of 2 x 4, and 44 2 x 4s, 6-feet long.

Step Two

The next step is to pre-drill and pre-screw. Make a drilling template, one for the end bits and another to attach the long bits of 2 x 4 to those end pieces, making your skeleton. Now, you can pre-drill all your holes and get the screws ready to go in.

Step Three

This is why you cut and pre-drill first—assembly time is dead simple.

Put your corner posts on the floor and mark the point where the shelf supports will go across them all. Use a tape measure or scrap wood to mark where your shelf heights will be.

The end brackets can now be attached to the corner posts. Do not forget that they should all be 21-inches long, so the total width with the side brackets is 24 inches.

Now comes the tricky part. First, you need to determine if your end brackets will be toward the inside or outside of the shelves. If you put them inside, you will need to cut some off-the-shelf pieces so they slide in; if you put them outside, the shelves will need to be notched.

Put the end pieces on their sides, spaced about eight feet apart, and then place your top support across them. That way, you can get the distance right. Do the same with the bottom support, and once you are happy, attach the supports. Repeat the operation with the middle supports, and it should be square.

Once your OSB has been cut or notched, you will need the patience to get the shelves to go in. If you notch it, cut them a bit larger. You could also consider cutting the shelves in half and fitting them that way, but you may need to add a center support depending on whether there is any sag.

Congratulations! Your shelving unit is ready to go into your root cellar and be stocked with all your fruit and vegetables.

Chapter 8: 8 Best Methods to Organizing a Root Cellar

Your root cellar is built, and you have even DIYed your storage shelves. All that is left to do is stock it. Many people will get excited at this stage and start piling in their vegetables without considering what they are doing.

If that is you, stop—right now!

Organizing a root cellar requires a great deal of thought and planning. Not all foods are happy together, and not all foods like the same temperatures. So, the next thing you will learn is how to organize your cellar, section by section. When you built your root cellar, you built it with its own temperature zones, whether you realized it or not. Working with those temperatures ensures that you can keep your food fresh for as long as possible, and proper organization means accessing your food quickly.

Method 1 — Using the Drawers

If your root cellar is equipped with drawers, you can at least use them to store certain vegetables and fruits. First, the drawers in the colder area of your root cellar can be used for fruit storage as these do much better in colder temperatures. Kept in high humidity and higher temperatures, fruits tend to break down very easily and rot. As such, dry, cooler temperatures are much better.

Vegetables prefer higher humidity because it stops them from drying out. Drawers in warmer parts of the root cellar can store broccoli, lettuce, carrots, and other produce. The higher the humidity level for these, the better. Some vegetables, such as spinach and cauliflower, are spritzed daily with water to keep them fresh in some grocery stores.

However, using drawers for storing produce does come with a warning — you must never mix fruits and vegetables in the same drawer. This is because every food type needs a specific humidity and temperature level, and storing them together will result in the loss of both fruits and vegetables and can cause mold to start growing.

Method 2 — The Upper Shelves

The upper shelves are best for food that you intend to eat fairly quickly. That includes ready-to-eat foods, leftovers, and drinks. These shelves are best because they are eye-level, and you see them straight away and are within easy reach. Obviously, if your root cellar is very tall and your upper shelves are above eye level, you will need to rethink that and use those you can see straight away.

Method 3 — The Middle Shelves

In any root cellar, the temperature around the middle shelves is the most constant, and that is where you should keep foods that must be kept cool but will not spoil so quickly. These may include eggs, cream, soft cheese, deli meats, and so on. Vegetables you can store on these shelves also include peppers, pumpkins, squash, sweet potatoes, and tomatoes.

Method 4 — The Lower Shelves

Down near the floor, the temperature is at its coldest, which is where spoilable foods need to go, such as chicken, fish, and other meats. This also prevents juices from dripping down onto other foods. Vegetables suitable for storage include potatoes, cabbage, cauliflower, dried beans, onions, and parsnips.

Method 5 — Keeping a Journal

When you first start a root cellar, you must keep a journal. That way, you will know what you have in storage at any time and where it is in the cellar. Information to put in your cellar journal includes:

- The date.
- The item stored.
- The quantity at the start of storage—this must be kept updated as you take stuff out.
- Other information regarding the food you consider important, including notes on storage techniques, whether it needs to be moved to a different part of the cellar, and so on.

The same applies to any foods that you choose to can for storage.

Method 6 – Keep Similar Foods Together

This applies to all foods, whether root vegetables, fruits, canned products, jars, or more. For example, keep all canned fruits, pie fillings, etc., in one place and tomato-based canned or bottled foods in another. Potatoes, beans, carrots, beets, etc., should be stored near one another. At the same time, fruits should be kept separate from the vegetables but stored in another area together. There are some exceptions, and it has all to do with ethylene gas—more details are provided later.

Method 7 – Rotate Your Food

One habit you must adopt is regularly checking your food, and this is where your journal comes in handy. If you have filled it in religiously, you will know what dates everything went in. Canned foods, bottled ones, cheeses, meats, dairy, etc., must be rotated to ensure that you use the oldest first—that way, things do not spoil and go to waste. With vegetables and fruits, they must be checked regularly, and anything that is going bad must be removed immediately. If something looks like it is beginning to spoil but is still edible, remove it for immediate use—in some cases, you can freeze what you salvage. Anything that has definitely gone off should be discarded, and all fruits and vegetables nearby checked carefully. These should also be wiped over—if one fruit or vegetable has gone moldy, it may have started spreading to others.

Method 8 – Store in Containers

Another way of storing your vegetables in a root cellar is in containers or bags, and one of the most common is plastic tubs. You can usually find five-gallon or larger tubs at fast food places, restaurants, supermarkets, and so on—simply go in and ask if they have any. More often than not, these are only going to be thrown away so you can put them to good use. Some of these containers will have lids—although they are generally single-use lids. That said, you can extend their use by cutting a few slots in the lid edge to fit it onto the container. These are ideal for storing many different fruits and vegetables, but you should cut air holes into the bottom and/or sides to ensure the air can circulate.
The second type of container you can use is wooden pallets. These are great for standing things like squash and pumpkins as they provide plenty of air circulation. Alternatively, you can build crates out of a series of pallets. By layering newspaper or straw between layers of vegetables, you can easily store large amounts in one place.
You can also use feed bags or burlap sacks. Feed bags are usually made from woven plastic and are breathable, ideal for storing food. They suit cabbages or apples layered with straw or leaves to keep them apart.
Cardboard boxes or wooden crates are also superb for storage. Some of these can be filled with sand and used to store carrots and other root vegetables. Make alternate layers of vegetables and sand until you reach the top.

Top Storage Tips

This chapter finishes with some other tips on storage and general information to help your storage organization go much smoother, ensuring better chances of success.

While proper storage is absolutely critical to success, there are other things you need to do. Otherwise, all your careful planning will go to waste.

Manage the Climate

As you have already learned, the climate in your root cellar is critical—that includes humidity, temperature, and ventilation. Most crops require a temperature between 32 and 40 degrees Fahrenheit and humidity of 90 to 95 percent. Others need warmer temperatures, between 50 and 60 degrees, with humidity of 60 to 70 percent. Root cellars with packed dirt floors are better than those with concrete floors because they ensure higher humidity. Again, humidity can be increased by using a humidifier or placing bowls of water on the floor.

Air the Cellar

Proper ventilation is essential to keeping odors out, slowing rotting and spoilage by evacuating ethylene gas, and regulating humidity and temperature. In that regard, ensuring you have adequate inlet and outlet pipes is the best guarantee of all.

Keeping Your Root Cellar Cool

With the following tips, you can ensure the best climate in your root cellar:

- Digging your root cellar at least ten feet (three meters) down ensures you reach complete temperature stability.
- Not digging your root cellar near big trees. The roots are not only tough to dig through, but they will also grow and crack the walls in your carefully dug root cellar.
- Use wood as far as possible for your storage as it does not conduct heat and cold like other materials.
- Stand your storage shelves, bins, etc., about 1 inch away from the wall to ensure proper air circulation.
- Have a packed earth floor rather than concrete.
- Ensure you install a hygrometer and thermometer to monitor temperature and humidity.
- Ensure adequate ventilation.

One Last Tip for Now

- *Keep the lights off.* If your root cellar has windows, make sure they are shaded. Lights should be kept off as much as possible since too much light can cause a loss of quality, and some vegetables may begin sprouting.

Root Cellar Ventilation and Ethylene Gas

Not having the right or adequate ventilation is one of the more common mistakes in designing and installing a root cellar. Most people are under the impression that food storage areas should be kept airtight to remain cold, but this is the fastest way for food to spoil.

This is by no means a good idea. Some foods will give off a gas known as ethylene. You cannot smell this gas, but it is the leading cause of food over-ripening and rotting in root cellars. Airtight areas can also be too humid, leading to excess water, which leads to the formation of mildew and mold.

You already know that you should have two vents in your cellar, one near the top of the room and one near the bottom. The bottom one allows the colder air in, while the top one vents out stale, warm air and ethylene gas.

If your room is around six by eight feet, you will get away using a 4-inch PVC pipe. Any larger, and the pipes need to be larger. All ventilation pipes should be covered in mesh to ensure animals and pests cannot get in, and they should be curved or angled so that debris, snow, or rain can't fall into the cellar.

Ethylene gas has been mentioned in this book several times, which tells you how important the subject is.

When some fruits ripen, particularly pears and apples, they give off this gas, which reduces the shelf life of other produce around them. It can cause early sprouting, mold, rotting, shrinking, yellowing, soft or tough skins, a bitter taste, and lots of other damage. To curb this phenomenon, vegetables and fruits that produce the gas must be stored separately from those that can be affected. Foods that can emit excess ethylene gas include:

- Apricots
- Apples
- Avocados
- Yellow bananas
- Cantaloupes
- Blueberries
- All citrus fruit except for grapefruit
- Figs
- Cranberries
- Grapes
- Guavas
- Honeydew melons

- Green onions
- Ripe kiwifruit
- Melons
- Mangoes
- Nectarines
- Mushrooms
- Papayas
- Okras
- Passion fruit
- Watermelon
- Tomatoes
- Persimmons
- Peppers
- Pears
- Quince
- Plantains
- Prunes
- Pineapple
- Plums

Fruits and vegetables susceptible to damage by ethylene gas are:
- Broccoli
- Asparagus
- Cabbage
- Brussels sprouts
- Cauliflower
- Carrots
- Cucumbers
- Chard
- Eggplant
- Escarole
- Endive
- Green beans
- Kiwifruit

- Lettuce
- Kale
- Florist greens
- Cut flowers
- Peas
- Parsley
- Peppers
- Romaine lettuce
- Sweet potatoes
- Watercress
- Potatoes
- Leafy greens
- Yams
- Spinach
- Squash
- Potted plants

10 Final Tips to Store Your Harvest

- Leave it as late in the season as you can to stock your root cellar. If possible, keep the produce chilled somewhere, perhaps your refrigerator, before you place it in your cellar.
- Some vegetables, like pumpkins, winter squash, potatoes, and onions, must be cured for several days before they are placed into storage. This must be done in warm temperatures and helps the skin to harden off, ensuring they last longer in storage.
- Do not wash vegetables before storing them; simply brush off any loose dirt. Your vegetables will store much better, and wet vegetables are more susceptible to rotting. Regarding vegetables with top foliage, like beets and carrots, the foliage should be clipped back to about an inch above the top, and they are best stored in peat moss or damp sand.
- Be careful when handling your vegetables during the harvest and storing process. Even the slightest rough touch can cause invisible bruising, leading to early decomposition and rot.
- Turnips and cabbages should be stored away from other food—their odor can taint everything else.

- Fruit can breathe, especially pears and apples. Those that produce ethylene gas should be individually wrapped in paper to slow down its release.
- Space your vegetables out on their shelves or trays for optimum freshness—when you heap them together, they can generate heat, speeding up the rate of decomposition.
- Check your produce regularly and remove anything that is going off.

86

Chapter 9: Troubleshooting Common Problems

While owning a root cellar should be fun, there are likely to be problems in any place where you store food. Be it mold, pests, or whatever, food storage is a magnet for problems. This chapter deals with some of the worst ones and provides effective solutions.

Tips for Root Cellar Success

Rodents

Wherever there is food, there are mice and rats, even in a root cellar. The trick to keeping them out is to stop them from accessing your root cellar in the first place, and the easiest way to do that is to block off their access points. Metal wire mesh is one of the best ways to go about this. Place it over anywhere these creatures can access your storage, including vents. If you struggle to keep mice out of your cellar, you may need to consider placing your storage off the ground. Just keep in mind that many rodents can climb, and if their prize is your food, they will stop at nothing. Later, we will explore some natural ways to repel rodents and other pests from your root cellar but, for now, keeping it clean will help. You may also need to consider laying traps along the walls—these must be checked at least once a day and any dead rodents removed immediately.

Rot

Another common issue in root cellars, inevitably, is rot. You might have heard the saying "one rotten apple spoils the barrel," and this could not be more true. But how do you stop it from happening? You cannot entirely stop it, but you can minimize its occurrence considerably:

- When you harvest your vegetables, be extra careful. Sort through your produce before storing it—anything that has been damaged during the harvest, i.e., cut with a fork or space, should be put to one side. Anything that has been bruised, put aside. If you drop something, such as an apple or potato, it will probably have an invisible bruise even if it does not look damaged. Put it aside as well. Only undamaged, blemish-free foods should be stored in your root cellar. Those damaged can either be used immediately or stored in another way, such as freezing or canning.

- Another mistake many people make is to wash their root vegetables before storing them—however tempting it might be, do not do this. Root vegetables store much better the way they come out of the ground, with their roots, stems, and soil intact. All you need to do is gently brush off any excess dirt and place them straight into storage. Washing vegetables draws the moisture out of them and precipitates their decomposition.
- Ensure any canned or bottled foods are stored with airtight lids. Before you decide to can or bottle anything, the containers and lids must be sterilized beforehand—even the slightest bit of contamination can spoil the contents.
- When you store your produce, put the largest ones at the back and the smallest first—these are more likely to go off quickly and should be used early.
- If your cellar has high humidity, check for condensation. When water begins dripping from the ceiling or running down the walls, it can get onto your produce, and they will begin to rot. Before you store your food, pretreat your cellar ceiling with disinfectant, something like chlorine, as this slows down diseases transmitted by dripping water.

As a cardinal rule, check your root cellar regularly. Any foods starting to wither, rot, or show signs of decomposition should be removed immediately.

Insects

This seems to be more of a problem where nuts and grains are stored, and since you have other food in your root cellar, it means you should never use chemical sprays or insecticides—ever. The best way to keep insects out of your root cellar is to have a tight-fitting door, all cracks sealed up, and insect mesh over the vents and drainage. Alternatively, you can scatter bay leaves around—insects hate these with a passion—or other herbs with a strong smell.

Sprouting Vegetables

If you notice that your vegetables are starting to sprout in your root cellar, it means something is wrong, and it typically comes down to one of three things:

- *Ethylene gas* — Look at where you have stored the vegetables that are sprouting. What other fruits or vegetables that give off excess ethylene are nearby? If so, move them. Also, inspect your ventilation system—is it adequate? Is it working? Have you got it in the right place? If you answer "no" to any or all of those, it is a sign that something needs adjusting in your cellar.
- *Too warm* — If the temperature is too warm, it can force vegetables into growing, which is not something you want in your cellar. Once a plant begins to grow again,

it will need to be consumed fairly quickly. To stop any others from sprouting, once again, check your ventilation system.
- *Too much light* — Do you leave the door open when you visit your root cellar? Are the windows covered? Do you leave a light on for long periods? The only way to stop vegetables from growing again is to keep them in the dark for as long as possible.

Frozen Produce

If your produce is freezing in your root cellar, this simply indicates that the temperature is way too low. First, check your thermometer. If the temperature is below freezing, you need to raise it. However, at this stage, you may already have lost much of your stored foods. Most vegetables will go mushy and rot when they freeze, making them unusable for anything. The second thing to check is what vegetables are frozen. If it is only those at the bottom, the air coming in through the inlet is too cold, meaning you most likely did not dig your root cellar deep enough. There is little you can do about that except emptying it and digging deeper. Don't forget that constant temperature stability is reached at around ten feet or three meters underground.

Produce Going Off Too Quickly

Did you open the door of your root cellar and get knocked back by the smell? Yes, your food is going off quickly, and the smell is quite distinct. So, what would make that happen? Simply put, it is down to the climate in your root cellar. The main culprits are moisture, light, air, temperature, and microbial growth.
One of the fastest causes of fresh food going off is damage caused by microorganisms, such as yeast, mold, and bacteria. However, this can only happen when the conditions are right—they need nutrients and water to grow and reproduce. Most fruits and vegetables have an average of 90 percent water content, making them the perfect target. Light is a serious enemy of fresh food in storage. Too much exposure and the outer layer of the vegetable of fruit will begin to spoil. This process is called photodegradation, and it leads to discoloration and a loss of flavor, proteins, and vitamins.
The one thing you must not do is store any vegetables or fruits wet or in an airtight container. In fact, a lack of air circulation will do nothing more than hasten decay. If your humidity levels are too high, you run the risk of water pooling on the produce, once again resulting in rot.

Lastly, the temperature is a major consideration, and getting it right is critical. Bear in mind that some vegetables like it cool, whereas others like it warmer. Extremes of temperature can cause significant problems—cold to the point of freezing, and the food begins to form ice crystals inside. These expand and break through the cell walls, causing discoloration and, in some cases, a slimy texture.

As such, one of the most important things to do is get your climate right on point before you start storing food. Once your cellar is full, use your thermometer and hygrometer to measure temperature and humidity. Using a notebook to record your results daily can give you an early warning when something is not right.

Mold

When your root cellar is working as it should be, it will be cool the whole year, and humidity levels will remain steady. However, one thing can affect all root cellars, whether underground, in a basement or garage, under the porch, or a simple barrel in the ground: mold. While you may think you have sealed your cellar properly, construction flaws or inadequate maintenance can lead to mold growing where you do not want it. If your root cellar is attached to your home or inside it, mold growth in the cellar can have a detrimental effect on the air you breathe. When mold forms in a cellar or cold storage, it is because condensation has formed. It may be due to warmer air seeping into the room in the summer months, usually because the door has not been sealed properly. When that warm air hits the cold surfaces in your cellar, such as the roof or poorly insulated walls, it forms condensation. This creates the perfect conditions for mold to develop. In a short time, that mold will spread to your produce or onto the containers your food is stored in, and within a few days, your entire crop is ruined—that is how quickly it can happen.

Your root cellar should have air vents, and these are one of the best tools at your disposal to control humidity. In turn, that helps you control the conditions and prevent mold growth—these air vents will keep the fresh air moving through your cellar and keep it dry.

However, that is not the only source of mold. You can introduce it into your cellar on the food you take in there. In that case, it does not matter how well your root cellar functions—once the mold is there, it will grow and spread to other food and your root cellar structure.

Now, if you suspect or can clearly see mold growing in your root cellar, you need to do something about it immediately. If left unchecked, mold can quickly spread to other areas, especially if your root cellar is attached to your home. Professional help will be needed to remove the mold and repair the damage already done in some cases.

What damage, you might ask?

First off, and most important, is the damage it can do to your health. This is more likely to affect those with respiratory diseases, weak immune systems, or allergies, but long-term exposure can also affect people with no underlying problems. It can lead to infections, asthma, bronchitis, allergic reactions, and more. Some of the common symptoms of mold exposure include:

- Sneezing
- Coughing
- Constantly fatigue
- Eye and throat irritation
- Headaches
- Skin rashes and irritation
- Nausea
- Breathing problems
- Nosebleeds

In any case, it is strongly recommended that if any of these symptoms manifest, you seek immediate medical advice and not just assume they are caused by mold.

Second is the damage it can do to the structural integrity of your house or root cellar. It can infest your walls and ceilings, turn into fungus, cause decay in wooden structures, and lead to wet and dry rot. If left untreated, you will end up with some pretty hefty structural repairs in the future.

Many people think that the onset of winter will kill off the mold growing in their cellar, but in reality, this is not the case. While colder temperatures can slow the growth and freeze mold, they do not dry out the mold spores. As such, the mold simply lies dormant, and when the temperatures warm up again, off it goes, growing fast and hard.

So, clearly, you must not wait for winter to set in and hope it will solve the problem for you. There are two things you can do. If the mold is confined to the root cellar and has only just started growing, you can strip everything out and thoroughly wash the walls, floors, shelves, etc., with a solution of diluted chlorine bleach. Alternatively, you can use hydrogen peroxide, diluted to a solution of three to ten percent, distilled white vinegar, or baking soda and borax. When you use these solutions, do not wipe them all off — leaving a little on the surfaces can help counteract future growth.

As an aside, if the mold is growing on a concrete surface, you cannot clean it yourself. Concrete is made using water, and when you add additional water to the surface to clean it, the water is drawn deeper into the structure. It takes the mold and bacteria with it, making the problem worse.

Generally speaking, if the mold covers about ten feet or more or is on concrete surfaces, you need to call in professional help, which is your second option. Professional mold specialists have the right products to remove the mold, identify the source, and fix the damage. They can also tend to air circulation issues or advise you on what to do to stop the problem from occurring again.

Preventing Mold in Your Root Cellar

Once again, it comes back to proper air circulation and ventilation. This must feel like the thousandth reminder, but that should tell you how important these aspects are in a successful root cellar.

Make sure you have adequate ventilation in place and that it is in the right place. The inlet vent should be near the bottom of your cellar, while the outlet should be near the top. Hot air rises and will be taken out of the room via this outlet pipe. Correct ventilation and sufficient air circulation can also regulate humidity and optimize air quality, removing the conditions mold needs to develop.

Check that your cellar has no air leaks in it other than your ventilation system. Cracks in the walls and gaps in the window or the door frames can all let warm air in, causing major problems. Again, your cellar should be at least ten feet down in the ground. Your inlet pipe will only draw air at the same temperature as outside—ten feet down is the constant temperature. Any imperfections need to be fixed immediately to stop the problem from occurring and leading to expensive mold removal specialists being called. It will also stop the food in your cellar from being destroyed.

Effective Tips to Keep Critters Away

Mice, rats, and other pests can get into just about anything. The smallest of holes is an invitation, and once one is in, you can pretty much guarantee they will invite their friends, family, and long-lost relatives to enjoy the feast!

To that end, here are some tips to help you keep them away from your precious storage supplies.

- **Avoid Excess Moisture**

  Rodents do not just need food to survive; they also need water. Therefore, when they look for somewhere to feed, they will always look for somewhere moist, so you must not allow excess moisture to pool in your root cellar.

  Also, consider storing food off the ground—there is less chance that rodents will get at it. Sometimes, if the area is moist, the rats and mice may pass through, and you will not even notice they have been there. By adding easily accessible food into the equation, you open the floodgates to destruction.

- **Eliminate Water and Food Smells**

Leading on from the previous tip, if your root cellar smells of food and/or water, you can guarantee the ultra-sensitive noses of rats and mice will pick up on them. This is why it is imperative to keep your root cellar clean, free of water, and free of food smells. Proper air circulation will help with this, but strong food smells will be carried into the air. By minimizing these smells, you can use other smells, such as those that deter rodents, to cover trace odors.

Rats and mice do not just look for food and water—they want nesting material. Therefore, leaving piles of newspaper, sawdust, and other materials lying around will attract them. If there is enough, you may even find the rodents building their nest right there in your cellar.

Mildew and dust also tip rats and mice off to the fact that the area is relatively undisturbed. That tells them they are safe, and that is when they start nesting—and multiplying. Fast.

- **Peppermint and Spearmint are Great Deterrents**

If you have ever grown mint in your garden, you know how invasive it can be. This is why many people choose to grow it in pots. Rats, mice, and other rodents detest the smell of mint because it irritates their noses and throats. You can do two things with that knowledge. First, if your root cellar is outdoors, plant mint around the perimeter. It will grow quickly, spreading into the available space and surrounding the cellar. Second, you can sprinkle mint leaves in your cellar, scattering them around the produce. If you use bins to keep your food in, chuck a few leaves in—they will not hurt the vegetables or fruit, and they will keep them safe from invasion.

Replace the leaves twice each week. The smell will stay strong enough to keep the rodents out, and it will mask any water or food odors.

One more thing you can do is boil up some mint leaves in water and put it in a spray bottle. Then, spray around your cellar regularly to provide an extra layer of protection and freshness.

- **Use Mothballs**

Yes, they do smell strong, but that is the idea. Sprinkling mothballs in the root cellar can deter rodents and snakes; they hate it and will avoid it as much as they can. This could be the one thing that keeps your cellar free of pests. At first, the smell may overwhelm you, but you will get used to it. You have a (pretty obvious) choice—
a strong smell in the root cellar or no produce because the mice, rats, and snakes have taken over and eaten it all.

While snakes will not eat your fruit and vegetables, they are attracted by the mice and rats. So, if you do not get rid of the rodents, you won't get rid of the snakes.

- **Get a Cat or Two**

Most cats are excellent mousers and will certainly help curb the presence of rodents. Allow cats to roam around the outside of your root cellar—any rodents that approach are likely to lose the battle or will be deterred from coming closer. When you enter your root cellar, let a cat or two in with you. If there are any rodents around, the cats will sort them out. Cats will also tell you if rats or mice have been in there—they can smell their scent and will alert you to their presence. Some cats will also go after moles, chipmunks, squirrels, rabbits, and other small creatures that might have taken a fancy to your root cellar.

- **Don't Run Away**

When you enter your root cellar and mice or rats are scurrying around, do not back out. This works for snakes, too. Most of these creatures prefer to be alone and are not happy to stay where there is a human presence. Make a noise, stand your ground, and they will be the first to back down.

You should also ensure you enter the root cellar a few times each week, even if you don't need anything. You can use it as an excuse to check your crops over or do a bit of cleaning—a regular presence will cause some critters to vacate the area permanently. And when you do go in to check on things, make some noise. Rattle food bins, move them around, anything to tell any hidden creatures you are there and that they should leave.

- **Set Some Traps**

This is not a good idea if you let cats or children into your root cellar. Rat or mouse traps are easily set with a little peanut butter, as most rodents are attracted to this. You should also have a few bigger traps, just in case you get anything larger than a rat in your cellar. Alternatively, small spring traps can be modified with nail boards on the metal bars, making it easier to catch rodents of various sizes.

Place your traps along the cellar walls—this is usually where the rodents run. You should secure the traps to the ground as larger rodents can run off with them still attached. Inspect your traps daily. If there are any caught, you need to dispose of them at once. If sadly they are still alive, it is kinder to put them out of their misery immediately, rather than letting them suffer for a long time.

You can also put poison bait down—although you run the risk of cats eating poisoned rodents.

Lastly, if you want a more humane method to keep them out of your cellar, invest in an ultrasonic repellent device.

- **Keep a Steel Rod or Wooden Pole Handy**

Never enter your cellar without a hoe, steel rod, or a large, heavy wooden pole. Why? Because you do not want to be caught unprepared if there are mice, rats, or snakes in there. If your food is stored in bins, in sawdust, sand, or straw, never put your hand in—lots of things can hide in there, and you don't want to be bitten. Instead, use a hoe to dig through to get your vegetables out. Poke around using a rod or pole to investigate anything alive or waiting to pounce on you.

Rats can grow to a foot and a half in length if the conditions are right, so make sure your rod is at least two or three feet long—you may need to lash out the rat with it, and you don't want to be too close.

- **Hardware Cloth**

Mice and rats struggle to chew through hardware cloth, so it is a good idea to wrap your bins and crates in it, stretching it across the tops. That said, you still should not just stick your hand in without checking—mice are crafty, and any chink in your armor is their way in.

Hardware cloth also makes a good layer of protection, which is why many people line their walls with it to stop pests from getting in. As it is made from flexible wire mesh, it's tough for most rodents to chew through, and those who use it claim great success.

- **Lock it Down**

One of the most important things you can do to keep pests out of your root cellar is to keep it all secure. Your door should be sturdy, and it must be secure enough to keep the outside world from getting in. However, you do need to ensure proper ventilation. Place hardware cloth over your ventilation pipes to allow air to enter and exit while preventing anything else from getting in.

Inside your root cellar, store your produce in chew-proof bins. You can use wooden or plastic containers where you do not have an issue with mice and rats, but these offer little deterrents. Rodents will even use chewed plastic to build their nests.

You may also want to consider other options, such as metal, cinderblock, or cement, where you have a problem. If you can get hold of them, metal ammo containers work fine, or you can weld or solder metal together to make your own. Whatever you use, ensure it has a tight-fitting or protective lid on it.

- **Guinea Fowl**

Last but not least is the often under-rated guinea fowl. Sure, they are loud, and yes, they will boss any other poultry you may have around. That said, when it comes to pest deterrents, they are one of the very best.

The best way to keep mice, rats, snakes, and other critters out of your root cellar is to remove them from your property, and that is where the guinea fowl will come into play. They are excellent hunters and will also eat bugs and ticks. Besides, they are a fantastic alarm system, and adding a few to your flock will ensure you have a much better chance of keeping pests away.

All in all, pest control in a root cellar is a tough job and an ongoing one. However, it is well worth the fight, and if you do not stay on top of things, all your hard work will most likely go to waste.

Chapter 10: Cleaning and Sanitizing a Root Cellar

The last thing worth discussing is cleaning your root cellar. This should be done twice a year, the first time in March or April and the second before storing your next harvest. Come the spring, most of your remaining root crops will have gone past their best limits for storage. Whatever you did not use must be consumed or discarded, depending on whether they are fine or going off. If you store potatoes, garlic, or onions, while these are probably still okay to eat, it should be done soon, or you need to plant them in the garden to produce a new crop.

If you have too many good vegetables left and cannot use them straight away, find another way of storing them. Potatoes, garlic, and onion can be turned into a lovely pan of scalloped potatoes! Use your vegetables for cooking up a batch of meals that you can freeze for another day.

If you have vegetables that can still be stored for a couple of months, move them out of the cellar. Ensure they are stored in burlap sacks or dark, ventilated containers while you do your spring cleaning. That way, they will not be exposed to the light, and the air can still circulate, keeping them fresh. Put canned and bottled foods to one side—you will read more on this below.

Once you have cleared all your food out of the cellar, remove any storage bins, crates, and boxes. Cardboard boxes may not be usable for another year; if not, discard them. It is best to burn them, just in case there are any bacteria or spots of mold growth on them. Reusable containers should be scrubbed out thoroughly. Use a weak bleach solution to kill off any bacteria and wash them out in boiling water. Leave them to dry naturally. Back into the root cellar, give it a good sweep. Clear up any dust, dirt, and debris from the shelves and the floor.

Now it is time to clean your shelves. Start at the top and work down, washing each one in hot soapy water. Rinse them off thoroughly with clean water and then spray them over with a kitchen disinfectant or a diluted chlorine bleach solution. You can make this with a teaspoon of water diluted in a quart of water. Leave it to dry. While cleaning, make sure you still have adequate ventilation.

Once your root cellar is cleared out, leave the doors open to air out for a few days. If the cellar still smells musty, run a fan in there for a few days to help evacuate the stale air. Before you store your next harvest in the autumn, go back in there, have a final sweep out, rewash your storage containers and close down your vents. You do not want the warmer summer air getting in. Now you are ready to start over.

As a side note, you can use your root cellar in the summer months to keep early fruits and vegetables cool when you don't have time to process them straight away. However, do not leave them in there for more than a few days.

Canned and Bottled Foods

Anything stored in jars, bottles, or otherwise preserved needs to be dealt with differently. When you began with your root cellar, you should have started a notebook detailing the dates each item was preserved and placed into storage. You should also have labeled each container with the date of preservation.

Your first job is to go through everything. Check for anything that has expired or gone off, and discard it in the garbage. Go by the dates on your containers or in your notebook—the earliest products should have been used first, so all you should have in storage are those stored later. However, if your system went awry, you may be left with old food—you really should not eat this unless it has been pickled. Dairy products are way past their "best by" date by now, unless they have only just been placed into storage. Also, dispose of any rusted, dented, or bulging cans and any foods with torn or broken packaging.

Now, you can deal with what is left.

Wipe down all jars, cans, bottles, etc., to get rid of any dirt, dust, or sticky residue that may be on them.

Restock your cellar using a FIFO system—First In, First Out. The older stuff should be used first, or else it will go off soon.

Organize your food by type and label your shelves.

Ensure the conditions in your storage cellar are right, with proper ventilation, air circulation, and humidity.

Maintenance

During your spring clean, you should check everything in your root cellar and make a note of any repairs, improvements, or upgrades that need to be made. If you used wood in any of the structures, check it for rot or damage—this needs to be replaced first.

Check the seals around your ventilation pipes and renew if necessary. Do the same with doors and windows and make sure any drainage issues are dealt with straight away.

When it comes time to start storing your new harvest, you need to ensure the right conditions in the root cellar. Over the summer, the temperature will rise and fall again as the nights draw in and the outside temperatures begin dropping. Once your cellar has been aired out after the spring clean, keep the door shut as much as you can.

Ensure you have sufficient storage containers and bags—buy new ones if you need to. Check that your old ones are in good condition, with no nails or loose bits sticking out. Check your ventilation covers are in place—if necessary, replace them. When the outdoor temperatures are low enough, open your vent covers.

Your root cellar is finally ready to start working for you again.

Conclusion

As you can see, building a root cellar is hard work, but it must be done right if you are to be successful. Putting in the time and effort to ensure your ventilation, temperature, and humidity are right will save you a lot of pain and headaches in the winter months.

Keep in mind that you do not have to go for a traditional root cellar if you don't want to. You may not have space or time, or it may be that this is your first time, and you want to start simple and see how it works before you decide to go all in on building a full root cellar at home.

Whichever type of root cellar you choose, make sure you follow the various tips provided in this guide, as it is the best way to ensure your success. The last thing you want is to bring in a huge harvest and store it all the way, only to find it goes rotten, or the mice and rats are happily enjoying the fruits of your labor.

Sure, root cellaring is a serious commitment, and you must be on the ball at all times. That said, it is also meant to be fun and a great way for you to make the most of what you grow or can buy at farmer's markets throughout the year. It's also a fantastic way to ensure that you eat healthy, organic food all year round and that you are set when unfortunate circumstances hit and stores run low.

All this book can encourage you to do now is to get out there, build your cellar, and have some fun.

Good luck!

www.ingramcontent.com/pod-product-compliance
Lightning Source LLC
Chambersburg PA
CBHW081418080526
44589CB00016B/2592